STECK-VAUGHN

TARGET Spelling 1020

Margaret Scarborough
Mary F. Brigham
Teresa A. Miller

STECK-VAUGHN
C O M P A N Y

A Subsidiary of National Education Corporation

Table of Contents

About the Authors

Margaret M. Scarborough teaches at Elizabeth Seawell Elementary School in Chapel Hill, North Carolina. Her master's degree was conferred by the University of North Carolina. Ms. Scarborough has taught kindergarten through sixth-grade students with special learning needs. She works collaboratively with regular classroom teachers, remedial reading teachers, speech and language pathologists, and behavioral therapists. She is a member of the Learning Disabilities Association of North Carolina and past president of the Orange County Association for Children and Adults with Learning Disabilities.

Mary F. Brigham is principal of McNair Elementary School in Fort Bragg, North Carolina. She has led language arts, early childhood, and remedial reading programs for the Fort Bragg Schools, in addition to having had varied teaching experience at all levels. Ms. Brigham earned her master's degree at the University of North Carolina at Chapel Hill, where she is currently enrolled in the doctoral program in educational administration.

Teresa A. Miller has taught children in Virginia, Vermont, and North Carolina. Her degrees in education are from the College of William and Mary, and the University of North Carolina at Chapel Hill. She has worked with both children and adults in a wide variety of educational settings.

Acknowledgments
Cover Design: Sharon Golden, James Masch
Cover Illustration: Terrell Powell
Interior Design and Production: Dodson Publication Services
Illustrators: Peg Dougherty, Jimmy Longacre

Staff Credits
Executive Editor: Elizabeth Strauss
Project Editor: Chris Boyd
Project Manager: Sharon Golden

Two-syllable words with *a-*

around	alone	above	awake
agree	avoid	afraid	amaze

A. Fill in each blank with a spelling word.

1. I am _afraid_ of the dark.

2. Let's choose a show we can _agree_ on.

3. Is your sister asleep or _awake_ ?

4. The dogs ran _around_ the house.

5. Did that magic card trick _amaze_ you?

6. She doesn't like to eat _alone_ .

7. We will turn left to _avoid_ the traffic jam.

8. The clouds floated _above_ the earth.

B. Circle the word that is the same as the top one.

agree	avoid	around	afraid	awake	amaze
apree	(avoid)	aruond	afriad	(awake)	amase
aqree	awoid	(around)	afnaid	amake	anaze
(agree)	aviod	arounb	(afraid)	awoke	(amaze)
agee	avid	aroond	afaid	amoke	ameze

C. Put an *X* on the word that is <u>not</u> the same.

1. around	around	ar~~ou~~nb	around	around
2. agree	agree	agre~~c~~	agree	agree
3. afraid	afraid	afraid	afraid	~~afnaid~~
4. awake	~~amake~~	awake	awake	awake

Name _Megan_

1

Two-syllable words with *a-*

around	alone	above	awake
agree	avoid	afraid	amaze

A. Write the spelling words in alphabetical (ABC) order.

1. *above*   2. *afraid*   3. *agree*   4. _____

5. _____   6. _____   7. _____   8. _____

B. Find the missing letters. Then write the word.

1. a   o   n   e   *alone*

2. a   r   o   d   *around*

3. a   a   e   *amaze*

C. Write the spelling words that rhyme with the words below.

1. bone   tone   *alone*

2. found   ground   *around*

3. love   glove   *above*

4. rake   make   *awake*

5. graze   daze   *amaze*

D. Fill in the boxes with the right words.

1. a v o i d

2. a m a z e

3.

4. a f r a i d

5.

6.

7.

8.

Two-syllable words with *a-*

| 1 |
| 2 |
| 3 |
| 4 |

| around | alone | above | awake |
| agree | avoid | afraid | amaze |

A. Match each spelling word with its antonym (opposite).

_____ **1.** agree   **a.** asleep

_____ **2.** above   **b.** fearless

_____ **3.** afraid   **c.** differ

_____ **4.** awake   **d.** below

_____ **5.** alone   **e.** seek

_____ **6.** avoid   **f.** together

B. Use spelling words to complete the story.

My sister and her friends were home _____ one night. They were

playing cards _____ the kitchen table. Suddenly they heard a noise.

It was coming from the back porch!

They were too _____ to move. My sister finally said, "Turn out

the lights." Then she moved slowly to the screen door and peered around to

see what was on the porch. She moved carefully, because she wanted to

_____ being seen by a prowler. She saw something white.

To my sister's surprise, it was our cat. He was batting at moths flying

_____ him on the screen door. That's where the noise was coming

from! My sister and her friends had a good laugh. They couldn't believe that

the cat's noise had scared them so much.

C. How many syllables does each spelling word have? _____

1
2
3
4

Two-syllable words with *a-*

around	alone	above	awake
agree	avoid	afraid	amaze

A. Use each spelling word in a sentence.

around _____

agree _____

alone _____

avoid _____

above _____

afraid _____

awake _____

B. Write a spelling word under each picture.

1. _____   2. _____   3. _____

C. A word that means the same as another word is called
a synonym. Write the correct spelling word beside its
synonym.

1. surprise _____   2. scared _____

3. atop _____   4. alert _____

D. Write a paragraph using one of the spelling words.

_____

_____

_____

Words with *-ket* and *-et*

rocket	jacket	pocket	socket
ticket	market	racket	closet

A. Fill in each blank with a spelling word.

1. Did you buy a _____ to the school play?

2. He wears a coat instead of a _____.

3. I have a new tennis _____.

4. Don't let a baby put its finger near the _____.

5. You can hang your coat in the _____.

6. I bought some tomatoes at the _____.

7. Our country sent a _____ to the moon.

8. I keep my wallet in my back _____.

B. Find the missing letters. Then write the word.

1. r o ___ ___ ___ ___   _____

2. ___ ___ r ___ ___ ___   _____

3. ___ l ___ ___ ___ ___   _____

C. Write the spelling words in alphabetical order.

1. _____ 2. _____ 3. _____ 4. _____

5. _____ 6. _____ 7. _____ 8. _____

D. Write a paragraph using one of the spelling words.

_____

_____

_____

Name _____

Words with *-ket* and *-et*

rocket	jacket	pocket	socket
ticket	market	racket	closet

A. **Write the correct spelling word beside each clue.**

_____ 1. what you use to hit tennis balls

_____ 2. what you buy to get into a concert or movie

_____ 3. a place where people can buy and sell things

_____ 4. the part of your clothes where money can go

_____ 5. a small room used for storage

_____ 6. a short coat

_____ 7. a kind of spaceship

_____ 8. an opening for an electric plug

B. **Use spelling words to complete the story.**

I play tennis every day after school. When I get home, I change into

shorts. If the weather is cool, I get my _____. Then I grab my

tennis _____ and some balls from the front hall _____ and

head for the courts.

I play for an hour or two with friends. Each day is different. Some days I

play like a champ. When I hit the ball over the net, it flies like a

_____. Other days I can barely hit the ball straight. That's okay,

though. Even when I'm not playing well, I love the game of tennis.

C. **Write three spelling words that rhyme with each other.**

_____   _____   _____

LESSON 2

Words with *-ket* and *-et*

rocket	jacket	pocket	socket
ticket	market	racket	closet

A. Complete these exercises with spelling words.

1. Which words contain the vowel *a*?

   _____   _____   _____

2. Which word begins and ends with the same letter?

   _____

3. Which words contain the letters *ock*?

   _____   _____   _____

B. Circle the word that is the same as the top one.

<u>jacket</u>	<u>market</u>	<u>rocket</u>	<u>closet</u>	<u>pocket</u>	<u>ticket</u>
gacket	marhet	racket	cloret	packet	tiket
jacket	markte	rochet	clotse	pocket	tichet
qacket	market	rockte	closet	pochet	tickel
jaket	manket	rocket	cloest	pockte	ticket
jacekt	markit	rockit	closte	picket	tickett

C. Divide each spelling word into syllables on the lines below.

1. rocket _____ _____   2. jacket _____ _____

3. pocket _____ _____   4. socket _____ _____

5. ticket _____ _____   6. market _____ _____

7. racket _____ _____   8. closet _____ _____

Name _____

Words with *-ket* and *-et*

rocket	jacket	pocket	socket
ticket	market	racket	closet

A. Write a spelling word under each picture.

 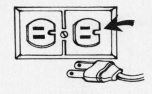 

1. _____   2. _____   3. _____

B. Match each spelling word with its synonym.

_____ **1.** jacket   **a.** store

_____ **2.** socket   **b.** cabinet

_____ **3.** market   **c.** coat

_____ **4.** closet   **d.** outlet

C. Write a paragraph using two of the spelling words.

_____

_____

_____

_____

_____

_____

_____

_____

D. All of the spelling words are _____.

(nouns, adjectives)

LESSON 3   Words with *-ther*

brother	mother	father	farther
other	another	bother	either

A. **Fill in each blank with a spelling word.**

1. Please don't _____ me while I'm working.

2. My mother and my _____ are my parents.

3. I've found _____ way to solve the problem.

4. His father is short, and his _____ is tall.

5. How much _____ must we drive?

6. The club will have a party _____ today or tomorrow.

7. She left her keys in her _____ coat.

8. I wish I had a _____ as well as a sister.

B. **Put an *X* on the word that is <u>not</u> the same.**

1. another	another	another	another	amother
2. either	either	eihter	either	either
3. farther	farther	farther	father	farther
4. other	other	othen	other	other
5. bother	bother	brother	bother	bother
6. father	farther	father	father	father

C. **Write the spelling words in alphabetical order.**

1. _____   2. _____   3. _____   4. _____

5. _____   6. _____   7. _____   8. _____

Name _____

9

Words with *-ther*

brother	mother	father	farther
other	another	bother	either

A. Circle the word that is the same as the top one.

brother	father	other	farther	another	either
bnother	farther	othen	farther	anothen	eithen
brother	fathar	othar	farthar	another	eithar
brothcr	feather	other	farthen	anather	eihter
brothen	father	otber	fether	anothar	either

B. Use spelling words to complete the story.

Have you been to a family reunion? It's a kind of party. It takes place when the relatives of _____ your mother or your _____ get together for a day or more of fun.

All the members of a family come from miles around to see each _____. They may bring lots of food. Some reunions are held near a lake or in a park. Those who want to can swim and play. Others can just sit and talk. When people in the same family learn about one _____, they learn things about themselves.

Sometimes there's a prize for the person who came _____ than all the others for the reunion. The oldest and youngest family members may also win a prize.

C. Which spelling words name members of a family?

_____   _____   _____

Words with *-ther*

brother	mother	father	farther
other	another	bother	either

A. Find the missing letters. Then write the word.

1. ___ n ___ ___ ___ ___ ___   _____

2. m ___ ___ ___ ___ ___   _____

3. ___ ___ r ___ ___ ___ ___   _____

4. b ___ ___ ___ ___ ___   _____

B. Write a paragraph using two of the spelling words.

_____

_____

_____

_____

_____

_____

C. Write the correct spelling word beside its antonym.

1. father _____   2. sister _____

3. nearer _____   4. neither _____

D. Write words that begin like each word below.

bother   father   mother   brother

_____   _____   _____   _____

_____   _____   _____   _____

Name _____

Words with *-ther*

brother	mother	father	farther
other	another	bother	either

A. Fill in the boxes with the right words.

1.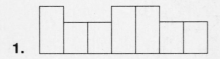

2.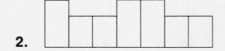

3.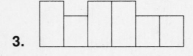

4.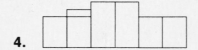

5.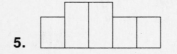

6.

B. Match each spelling word with the right clue.

_____ 1. farther   **a.** a boy with a sister

_____ 2. brother   **b.** one more

_____ 3. either   **c.** this one or the other one

_____ 4. another   **d.** more distant

C. Divide each spelling word into syllables on the lines below.

1. brother _____ _____   2. another _____ _____ _____

3. other _____ _____   4. mother _____ _____

5. father _____ _____   6. farther _____ _____

7. either _____ _____   8. bother _____ _____

Homonyms

do	knight	sight	wade
dew	night	site	weighed

A. Fill in each blank with a spelling word.

1. The moon comes up at _____.

2. Do you like to _____ in the water?

3. I _____ more last year than I do now.

4. We watched the bird until it flew out of _____.

5. The _____ rode off to battle on a white horse.

6. At morning there's _____ on the ground.

7. This corner will be the _____ of a new school.

8. What game _____ you like to play the most?

B. Complete these exercises with spelling words.

1. Write the words that are nouns.

_____ _____ _____

_____ _____

2. Which word begins with a silent letter? _____

3. Write the words that end with silent *e*.

_____ _____

4. Some of the words are verbs. Write one of them. _____

C. Write the spelling words in alphabetical order.

1. _____ **2.** _____ **3.** _____ **4.** _____

5. _____ **6.** _____ **7.** _____ **8.** _____

Name _____

LESSON 4

Homonyms

do	knight	sight	wade
dew	night	site	weighed

A. **Write the correct spelling word beside each clue.**

_____ 1. position or place of something

_____ 2. the darkness between evening and morning

_____ 3. power of seeing, or something worth seeing

_____ 4. a gallant man who serves his king

_____ 5. to carry out or perform

_____ 6. the moisture seen on grass in the morning

B. **Use each spelling word in a sentence.**

night _____

dew _____

site _____

knight _____

sight _____

wade _____

weighed _____

C. **Write a spelling word under each picture.**

1. _____   2. _____   3. _____

14

Homonyms

do	knight	sight	wade
dew	night	site	weighed

A. Circle the word that is the same as the top one.

dew	knight	night	site	wade	weighed
dem	kright	right	stie	wabe	wieghed
deu	knight	kihgt	seit	wade	weighd
dwe	knihgt	night	sete	waed	weighed
dew	kight	nithg	site	wead	weighde

B. Use spelling words to complete the story.

My uncle took me fishing last summer. We awoke in the middle of the

_____, dressed, and loaded our gear into the car.

We got to the lake at six o'clock in the morning. The sun was just

coming up. It was a beautiful _____. Steam was rising off the

water, and drops of _____ on the grass sparkled in the sunlight.

We carried our fishing gear down to the lake.

We got our poles ready and began to fish. After about two hours, I

caught a big fish. We took it home and put it on the scales. It

_____ ten pounds! The fish made a fine supper for us.

C. Find the missing letters. Then write the word.

1. ___ n ___ ___ ___ ___   _____

2. w ___ ___ ___ ___ ___ ___   _____

3. n ___ ___ ___ ___   _____

Homonyms

do	knight	sight	wade
dew	night	site	weighed

A. Write the correct spelling word beside its synonym.

1. moisture _____   2. darkness _____

3. view _____   4. place _____

B. Fill in the boxes with the right words.

1. 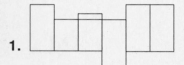   2. 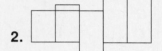   3.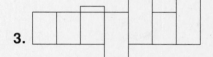

C. Find the hidden words on the list.

do	knight	sight	wade	other
dew	night	site	weighed	bother
rocket	jacket	pocket	socket	agree
ticket	market	racket	closet	awake

```
l  u  o  n  e  i  j  a  w  o  t  h  e  r
b  u  y  d  e  w  a  d  e  n  k  h  p  s
r  o  c  k  e  t  c  m  i  y  n  i  y  m
a  w  l  y  n  i  k  a  g  o  i  n  b  a
c  s  o  s  i  a  e  r  h  p  g  e  o  t
k  t  s  i  g  h  t  k  e  o  h  a  t  i
e  f  e  t  h  o  r  e  d  c  t  r  h  c
t  r  t  e  t  o  o  t  e  k  e  m  e  k
a  w  a  k  e  d  a  g  r  e  e  o  r  e
n  a  n  o  s  o  c  k  e  t  v  r  y  t
```

16

Silent *e* words with *-ing*

coming	using	living	biting
having	loving	hoping	making

A. Fill in each blank with a spelling word.

1. Are you _____ a good time?

2. Plants and animals are _____ things.

3. I was _____ that I would see you.

4. She's _____ a birthday cake for me.

5. Our dog keeps _____ the baby's toys.

6. His grandfather is a kind and _____ man.

7. We've been _____ the same toothpaste for years.

8. I am _____ to your party tonight.

B. Put an *X* on the word that is <u>not</u> the same.

1.	coming	coming	coming	coning	coming
2.	making	makimg	making	making	making
3.	loving	loving	loving	loving	living
4.	having	having	hawing	having	having

C. Find the missing letters. Then write the word.

1. ___ ___ p ___ ___ ___   _____

2. ___ ___ t ___ ___ ___   _____

3. m ___ ___ ___ ___ ___   _____

4. h a ___ ___ ___ ___   _____

Name _____

Silent *e* words with *-ing*

coming	using	living	biting
having	loving	hoping	making

A. Write the root word of each spelling word.

1. coming *come*
2. using _____
3. living _____
4. biting _____
5. having _____
6. loving _____
7. hoping _____
8. making _____

B. Write the correct spelling word beside its synonym.

1. chewing _____
2. wishing _____
3. forming _____
4. arriving _____

C. Change the spelling words to the past tense by adding *ed* to the root word. Use each new word in a sentence.

live _____

hope _____

use _____

D. Write the spelling words in alphabetical order.

1. _____
2. _____
3. _____
4. _____
5. _____
6. _____
7. _____
8. _____

Silent *e* words with *-ing*

coming	using	living	biting
having	loving	hoping	making

A. Write the correct spelling word beside its past tense form.

1. bit _____

2. used _____

B. Write the correct spelling word beside its antonym.

1. going _____

2. hating _____

3. dying _____

4. destroying _____

5. doubting _____

6. needing _____

C. Write each word three times.

having _____ _____ _____

biting _____ _____ _____

using _____ _____ _____

making _____ _____ _____

hoping _____ _____ _____

loving _____ _____ _____

coming _____ _____ _____

living _____ _____ _____

D. Write the spelling words that rhyme with the words below.

1. taking   baking   _____

2. roping   moping   _____

3. fighting   lighting   _____

Name _____

LESSON 5

1
2
3
4

Silent *e* words with *-ing*

| coming | using | living | biting |
| having | loving | hoping | making |

A. **Use spelling words to complete the story.**

Tomorrow I'm _____ a big birthday party. I'm _____

we'll have a cake this year.

On the morning of last year's party, my sister was _____ my

cake. As she was putting the icing on it, she looked up to see our dog

_____ into the kitchen. He smelled the cake. Then he leaped onto

the table and started _____ into it.

My sister yelled at the dog, but it was too late. The cake was all gone.

We had to laugh at our dog. He looked so funny with cake on his whiskers.

At the party, we stuck candles in the ice cream, and someone lit them. While

I was blowing them out, I wished for a cake on my next birthday.

B. **Use each spelling word in a sentence.**

coming _____

biting _____

having _____

loving _____

making _____

hoping _____

using _____

living _____

Words with *-ing*

dropping	pinning	hopping	canning
shipping	humming	stripping	stopping

A. Fill in each blank with a spelling word.

1. What's that tune he's _____?

2. Are you _____ or freezing those green beans?

3. We're _____ those boxes by truck.

4. Let's try _____ it together with safety pins.

5. Once he gets started, there's no _____ him.

6. She'll start by _____ the paint off the chair.

7. In the race, we were _____ on one foot.

8. The children were _____ crumbs to mark the trail.

B. Make new words from the letters in the words below.

shipping   stripping   dropping

_____   _____   _____

_____   _____   _____

C. Write the spelling words in alphabetical order.

1. _____   2. _____   3. _____

4. _____   5. _____   6. _____

7. _____   8. _____

D. Find the missing letters. Then write the word.

1. ___ i ___ ___ ___ ___ ___   _____

2. s ___ o ___ ___ ___ ___ ___   _____

Words with -ing

dropping	pinning	hopping	canning
shipping	humming	stripping	stopping

A. Write the root word of each spelling word.

1. dropping _____
2. pinning _____
3. hopping _____
4. canning _____
5. shipping _____
6. humming _____
7. stripping _____
8. stopping _____

B. Write the spelling words that rhyme with the words below.

1. winning   spinning   _____
2. panning   fanning   _____
3. stopping   dropping   _____
4. tipping   stripping   _____
5. strumming   drumming   _____

C. Write a paragraph using two of the spelling words.

_____

_____

_____

_____

_____

_____

_____

Words with *-ing*

dropping	pinning	hopping	canning
shipping	humming	stripping	stopping

A. Use spelling words to complete the puzzle.

Across

3. letting fall down

5. holding with pins

6. short jumping

Down

1. quitting

2. sending by ship

4. putting in cans

B. Write words that begin like each word below.

<u>sh</u>ipping   <u>str</u>ipping   <u>st</u>opping   <u>dr</u>opping

_____   _____   _____   _____

_____   _____   _____   _____

Name _____

LESSON 6 Words with *-ing*

| dropping | pinning | hopping | canning |
| shipping | humming | stripping | stopping |

A. Use spelling words to complete the story.

My grandmother had been _____ her own vegetables for

most of her life. Five years ago, she tried something new. She made grape

jelly. The grapes grow wild in her yard. Her jelly was so good that people

began _____ in our town to buy jars of it.

Now her jelly is famous. She sells it to people all over the world. This

year, she's even _____ a box of it to China.

B. Write the spelling words that rhyme with the words below.

shopping   tipping

_____   _____

_____   _____

_____

C. Sometimes the words "hopping" and "hoping" are confused with each other. Use each word correctly in a sentence.

hopping _____

hoping _____

D. Write a spelling word under each picture.

1. _____   2. _____   3. _____

Silent *e* words with *-er*

wiper	shaver	voter	glider
diner	giver	skater	ruler

A. Fill in each blank with a spelling word.

1. Use the _____ to make a straight line.

2. Does he use a razor or an electric _____?

3. I am a good roller _____.

4. Every _____ is important on election day.

5. The windshield _____ is broken.

6. I ate my lunch at a _____.

7. A type of plane without an engine is a _____.

8. It's better to be a _____ than a taker.

B. Find the missing letters. Then write the word.

1. ___ ___ p ___ ___   _____

2. ___ k ___ ___ ___ ___   _____

3. ___ o ___ ___ ___   _____

4. ___ ___ v ___ ___   _____

C. Match each spelling word with its synonym.

_____	1. giver	a.	razor
_____	2. diner	b.	donor
_____	3. shaver	c.	restaurant
_____	4. ruler	d.	plane
_____	5. glider	e.	measurer

Name _____

Silent *e* words with *-er*

wiper	shaver	voter	glider
diner	giver	skater	ruler

A. Use spelling words to answer these riddles.

1. What can be this and can also measure lines?

   _____

2. What can be a person who is eating and a place to eat?

   _____

3. What can be someone who glides or an airplane with no engine?

   _____

B. Use spelling words to complete the story.

Today is election day. At the _____ where I eat, I saw a big sign. It said "Every _____ should go to the polls and vote."

We're electing a new president for our country. Many countries in the world have presidents. Some have a king or a queen for a _____. And there are other kinds of leaders.

Our president is called our "chief executive officer." I think it would be exciting to be the head of a nation. But there would be many duties and problems to solve.

C. All of the spelling words are _____.
(nouns, verbs, adjectives)

Silent *e* words with *-er*

wiper	shaver	voter	glider
diner	giver	skater	ruler

A. Write the root word of each spelling word.

1. wiper _____   **2.** shaver _____

3. diner _____   **4.** giver _____

5. voter _____   **6.** skater _____

7. glider _____   **8.** ruler _____

B. Write the correct spelling word beside each clue.

_____ **1.** a place to eat

_____ **2.** something used for wiping

_____ **3.** a tool that cuts hair on the face

_____ **4.** a strip with a straight edge for measuring

_____ **5.** a plane with no motor

_____ **6.** one who skates

C. Change the spelling words to the past tense by adding *ed* to the root word. Use each new word in a sentence.

wipe _____

skate _____

vote _____

shave _____

glide _____

rule _____

Name _____

Silent *e* words with *-er*

wiper	shaver	voter	glider
diner	giver	skater	ruler

A. Write each word three times.

shaver _____ _____ _____

giver _____ _____ _____

voter _____ _____ _____

ruler _____ _____ _____

skater _____ _____ _____

wiper _____ _____ _____

B. Write the spelling words that have the long *i* sound.

1. _____ 2. _____ 3. _____

C. Write words that begin like each word below.

skater shaver glider giver

_____ _____ _____ _____

_____ _____ _____ _____

_____ _____ _____ _____

_____ _____ _____ _____

D. Sometimes the words "diner" and "dinner" are confused with each other. Use each word correctly in a sentence.

diner _____

dinner _____

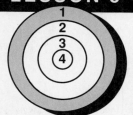

Homonyms

mail	whole	wrap	buy
male	hole	rap	by

A. Fill in each blank with a spelling word.

1. I have a _____ in my sock.

2. We'll need tape and paper to _____ the present.

3. What did you _____ in Mexico?

4. We walked _____ the stream.

5. I heard a _____ on the window.

6. A _____ goose is called a gander.

7. Our family ate a _____ pumpkin pie.

8. Did you get the _____ from the post office box?

B. Find the missing letters. Then write the word.

1. ___ h ___ ___ ___   _____

2. ___ ___ y   _____

3. ___ ___ i ___   _____

4. ___ r ___ ___   _____

C. Write the correct spelling word beside its synonym.

1. entire _____   2. knock _____

3. purchase _____   4. send _____

5. man _____   6. cover _____

D. Write the spelling words that can be verbs.

_____   _____   _____   _____

Name _____

Homonyms

mail	whole	wrap	buy
male	hole	rap	by

A. Find the hidden words on the list.

mail	whole	wrap	buy	father
male	hole	rap	by	humming
wiper	ruler	voter	glider	alone
diner	giver	skater	shaver	closet

```
c f r e a d e r s h a v e r n
l u l a w i p e r o n e b u y
o t g h m e s p u l a e y s e
s u i u e m m a l e p v g a s
e r v m t a r t e w h o l e k
t e e m d i n e r o p t i e a
o s r i l l e r a n d e d a t
a l o n e w r a p e a r e t e
r o l g u g h f a t h e r a r
```

B. Match each spelling word with its antonym.

_____ 1. male   a. part

_____ 2. whole   b. sell

_____ 3. buy   c. female

_____ 4. wrap   d. uncover

C. Write the spelling words in alphabetical order.

1. _____   2. _____   3. _____   4. _____

5. _____   6. _____   7. _____   8. _____

Homonyms

mail	whole	wrap	buy
male	hole	rap	by

A. Use spelling words to complete the story.

At holiday time in our small town, the children _____ gifts for

each other at the store. The butcher gives them a big roll of white paper.

They spend a _____ day painting and coloring the paper. Then they

_____ their gifts for each other in it.

B. Circle the word that is the same as the top one.

hole	male	wrap	mail	buy	whole
hale	mael	wrab	mial	buy	wnole
hoel	male	wnap	nail	bay	wrote
holl	mate	warp	mail	bug	whole
hole	meal	wrap	mile	boy	whale

C. Write a paragraph using two of the spelling words.

_____

_____

_____

_____

_____

_____

_____

Name _____

Homonyms

| mail | whole | wrap | buy |
| male | hole | rap | by |

A. Match each spelling word with the right clue.

_____ 1. by   **a.** a hollow place

_____ 2. whole   **b.** a boy or man

_____ 3. male   **c.** near or next to

_____ 4. mail   **d.** letters and packages

_____ 5. hole   **e.** entire or complete

_____ 6. rap   **f.** to purchase something

_____ 7. buy   **g.** to cover completely

_____ 8. wrap   **h.** a sharp blow

B. Write the spelling words that contain a silent consonant.

_____   _____

C. Add *ing* to the spelling words below. Then use each new word in a sentence.

wrap _____

rap _____

D. Write the spelling words that have a silent *e*.

_____   _____   _____

Words with *-er*

zipper	dropper	clipper	jogger
slipper	winner	chopper	shopper

A. Fill in each blank with a spelling word.

1. The _____ of the game has the most cards.

2. Do you have a nail _____?

3. The _____ behind me bought six gallons of milk.

4. I've finished the skirt except for the _____.

5. He uses a _____ to cut up vegetables.

6. We fed the baby bird from a medicine _____.

7. I lost my left _____.

8. The _____ ran two miles every day.

B. Write the root word of each spelling word.

1. zipper _____   2. slipper _____

3. dropper _____   4. winner _____

5. clipper _____   6. chopper _____

7. jogger _____   8. shopper _____

C. Write a spelling word under each picture.

1. _____   2. _____   3. _____

Name _____

LESSON 9

1
2
3
4

Words with -er

zipper	dropper	clipper	jogger
slipper	winner	chopper	shopper

A. Complete these exercises with spelling words.

1. Which words contain the vowels *i* and *e*?

_____   _____

_____   _____

2. Which word begins with *sh*? _____

B. Add the suffix (ending) *ing* to each root word below. Use each new word in a sentence.

jog _____

shop _____

win _____

chop _____

zip _____

drop _____

C. Match each spelling word with the right clue.

_____ **1.** winner   **a.** runner

_____ **2.** jogger   **b.** a cutting tool

_____ **3.** zipper   **c.** a person who visits a store

_____ **4.** chopper   **d.** a fastener with metal teeth

_____ **5.** slipper   **e.** champion

_____ **6.** shopper   **f.** a bedroom shoe

LESSON 9

Words with *-er*

zipper	dropper	clipper	jogger
slipper	winner	chopper	shopper

A. Write the spelling words in alphabetical order.

1. _____   2. _____   3. _____

4. _____   5. _____   6. _____

7. _____   8. _____

B. Put an *X* on the word that is <u>not</u> the same.

1. zipper	zipper	zibber	zipper	zipper
2. slipper	stipper	slipper	slipper	slipper
3. winner	winner	winner	wiuuer	winner
4. jogger	jogger	jogger	jogger	joggen
5. chopper	chapper	chopper	chopper	chopper
6. dropper	dropper	dropper	dropper	droppen
7. clipper	clipper	cliqqer	clipper	clipper
8. shopper	shoppen	shopper	shopper	shopper

C. Use spelling words to complete the story.

The cool day was just right for a race. I've been a _____ for

a long time, but I've never run in a race. I was nervous at the starting line.

The _____ on my jacket got stuck, but I just forgot about my

jacket and ran as hard as I could. I wasn't a _____ that day, but

it felt good to be part of the race.

Name _____

35

LESSON 9

Words with *-er*

zipper	dropper	clipper	jogger
slipper	winner	chopper	shopper

A. Write words that begin like each word below.

chopper   slipper   clipper   jogger

_____   _____   _____   _____

_____   _____   _____   _____

_____   _____   _____   _____

_____   _____   _____   _____

B. Fill in the boxes with the right words.

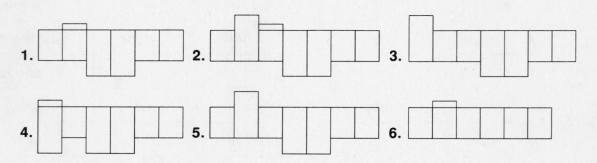

C. Match each spelling word with its synonym.

_____ **1.** winner   **a.** cutter

_____ **2.** zipper   **b.** customer

_____ **3.** jogger   **c.** snipper

_____ **4.** shopper   **d.** champion

_____ **5.** clipper   **e.** runner

_____ **6.** chopper   **f.** fastener

Silent *e* words with *-ed*

| scraped | hiked | chased | closed |
| timed | used | filed | moved |

A. Fill in each blank with a spelling word.

1. My sister and I _____ up the mountain.

2. The dog _____ the cat down the street.

3. He _____ the door on his finger.

4. The judge _____ the swimmer at forty seconds.

5. They _____ the names in alphabetical order.

6. She _____ two eggs in the cake.

7. I _____ from the city to the country last year.

8. The girl _____ her knee when she fell.

B. Find the missing letters. Then write the word.

1. ___ s ___ ___   _____

2. ___ ___ l ___ ___   _____

3. ___ h ___ ___ ___ ___   _____

4. ___ l ___ ___ ___ ___   _____

C. Write the spelling words in alphabetical order.

1. _____ 2. _____ 3. _____

4. _____ 5. _____ 6. _____

7. _____ 8. _____

D. All of the spelling words are _____.
(nouns, verbs, adjectives)

Name _____

LESSON 10
Silent *e* words with *-ed*

scraped	hiked	chased	closed
timed	used	filed	moved

A. Write the root word of each spelling word.

1. scraped _____   2. hiked _____

3. chased _____   4. closed _____

5. timed _____   6. used _____

7. filed _____   8. moved _____

B. Write a paragraph using two of the spelling words.

_____

_____

_____

_____

_____

_____

_____

_____

C. Fill in the boxes with the right words.

1.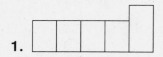

2.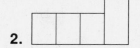

3.

4.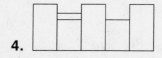

5.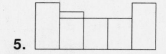

6.

38

Silent *e* words with *-ed*

scraped	hiked	chased	closed
timed	used	filed	moved

A. Use spelling words to complete the story.

The boy scouts at our school planned their campout well this year. They

learned from last year's mistakes. They know to be more prepared this time.

Last year, they didn't practice putting up their tents before the campout.

This year, they practiced often and even _____ each other with

a stopwatch. They also _____ up and down hills to get in

better shape.

The scouts _____ up all their matches trying to start a

cooking fire last year. This time, they learned the right way to start a fire

and keep it going. They made a list of all the supplies they'll need, so they

won't forget anything. Then the scouts made a copy of the list and

_____ it away. They should have a great time this year.

B. Write each word three times.

scraped _____ _____ _____

timed _____ _____ _____

hiked _____ _____ _____

chased _____ _____ _____

filed _____ _____ _____

closed _____ _____ _____

used _____ _____ _____

moved _____ _____ _____

Name _____

LESSON 10   Silent *e* words with *-ed*

scraped	hiked	chased	closed
timed	used	filed	moved

A. Match each spelling word with its synonym.

_____ **1.** timed   **a.** shut

_____ **2.** moved   **b.** rubbed

_____ **3.** closed   **c.** followed

_____ **4.** used   **d.** spent

_____ **5.** scraped   **e.** walked

_____ **6.** chased   **f.** clocked

_____ **7.** hiked   **g.** went

_____ **8.** filed   **h.** stored

B. Circle the word that is the same as the top one.

<u>timed</u>	<u>scraped</u>	<u>used</u>	<u>chased</u>	<u>closed</u>	<u>moved</u>
tined	soraped	nsed	cnased	closeb	moved
timeb	scraped	useb	crased	clased	moned
timed	scrapped	used	chaseb	closde	moveb
timmed	scnapped	uzed	chased	closed	maved
tired	scruped	uzeb	charsed	closet	movid

C. Sometimes the words "filed" and "filled" are confused with each other. Use each word correctly in a sentence.

filed _____

filled _____

40

Words with *-ed*

ripped	shipped	stepped	scrubbed
hopped	canned	dropped	slammed

A. Fill in each blank with a spelling word.

1. We're eating food this winter that we _____ last summer.

2. When I _____ my glasses, they broke.

3. The door _____ on her finger.

4. The sink was _____ every morning.

5. My shirt is so old that it _____ in the wash.

6. The rabbit _____ across the road.

7. The coal was _____ by train.

8. The sailor _____ into the boat carefully.

B. Write the spelling words in alphabetical order.

1. _____   2. _____   3. _____

4. _____   5. _____   6. _____

7. _____   8. _____

C. Fill in the boxes with the right words.

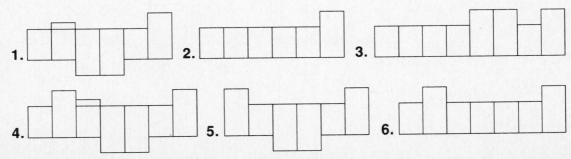

Name _____

LESSON 11

Words with -ed

ripped	shipped	stepped	scrubbed
hopped	canned	dropped	slammed

A. Write the root word of each spelling word.

1. ripped _____   2. shipped _____

3. stepped _____   4. scrubbed _____

5. hopped _____   6. canned _____

7. dropped _____   8. slammed _____

B. Complete these exercises with spelling words.

1. Which word begins and ends with the same letter?

   _____

2. Which words contain the vowel *a*?

   _____   _____

3. Which is the longest word? _____

C. Add the suffix *ing* to each root word below. Use each new word in a sentence.

scrub _____

drop _____

rip _____

slam _____

step _____

hop _____

ship _____

can _____

42

Words with *-ed*

ripped	**shipped**	**stepped**	**scrubbed**
hopped	**canned**	**dropped**	**slammed**

A. Write the spelling words that rhyme with the words below.

1. slipped   tripped   _____

2. shopped   flopped   _____

3. fanned   banned   _____

B. Match each spelling word with its synonym.

_____ **1.** ripped   **a.** sent

_____ **2.** scrubbed   **b.** walked

_____ **3.** stepped   **c.** cleaned

_____ **4.** shipped   **d.** jumped

_____ **5.** hopped   **e.** tore

_____ **6.** canned   **f.** preserved

C. Put an *X* on the word that is <u>not</u> the same.

1. ripped	riped	ripped	ripped	ripped
2. shipped	shipped	shipped	snipped	shipped
3. stepped	stepped	steeped	stepped	stepped
4. scrubbed	scnubbed	scrubbed	scrubbed	scrubbed
5. dropped	dropped	dropped	dropped	droppeb
6. slammed	slammed	slamed	slammed	slammed
7. canned	canned	caned	canned	canned
8. hopped	hopped	hopped	hopped	hoped

Name _____   **43**

LESSON 11   Words with *-ed*

ripped	shipped	stepped	scrubbed
hopped	canned	dropped	slammed

A. Use spelling words to complete the story.

Yesterday was a bad day for my brother. While he was walking to

school, he _____ a heavy book on his foot. It hurt so much, he

_____ the rest of the way to school.

Later that day, he _____ his locker door on his finger by

accident. Then, as he was leaving for home, he fell down the steps and

_____ a hole in his jeans. My brother says he's going to bed for

the rest of the day. I hope tomorrow is a better day for him.

B. Match each spelling word with the right clue.

_____ 1. canned   **a.** how a package could be sent

_____ 2. slammed   **b.** what the kangaroo did

_____ 3. ripped   **c.** how the door was shut by the wind

_____ 4. shipped   **d.** what was done to beans to store them on a shelf

_____ 5. hopped   **e.** what the sheet did when it was pulled apart

C. Sometimes the words "hoped" and "hopped" are confused with each other. Use each word correctly in a sentence.

hoped   _____

hopped   _____

44

LESSON 12

Homonyms

| wear | weather | which | heard |
| where | whether | witch | herd |

A. Fill in each blank with a spelling word.

1. Can you name the movie that has a good _____ in it?

2. _____ are you going on vacation?

3. We saw a _____ of cattle on the ranch.

4. Have you heard the _____ report for tomorrow?

5. What are you going to _____ to the party?

6. I don't know _____ to go or stay.

7. _____ pie is your favorite?

8. Have you _____ my newest joke?

B. Fill in the boxes with the right words.

1. 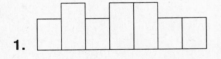   2. 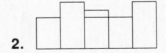   3.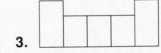

4. 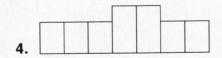   5. 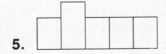   6.

7. 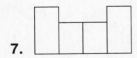   8.

C. Write the spelling words that have two syllables.

_____   _____

Name _____

Homonyms

wear	weather	which	heard
where	whether	witch	herd

A. Write a paragraph using two of the spelling words.

_____

_____

_____

_____

_____

_____

_____

_____

B. Use spelling words to complete the puzzle.

Across

1. what is done with a mask

4. I don't know ___ or not to go.

5. listened to

Down

1. rain, storms, sunshine

2. a group of cows

3. at or in what place

LESSON 12 — Homonyms

wear	weather	which	heard
where	whether	witch	herd

A. Write the spelling words in alphabetical order.

1. _____ 2. _____ 3. _____

4. _____ 5. _____ 6. _____

7. _____ 8. _____

B. Match each spelling word with the right clue.

_____ 1. where   a. what you did with your ears

_____ 2. weather   b. to have on the body, or to use up

_____ 3. witch   c. a group of cows or sheep

_____ 4. heard   d. at, in, or to what place

_____ 5. wear   e. a woman who casts spells in fairy tales

_____ 6. herd   f. rain, hail, sunshine, or snow, for example

_____ 7. which   g. if

_____ 8. whether   h. what one out of a group

C. Write a spelling word under each picture.

1. _____ 2. _____ 3. _____

Name _____

Homonyms

wear	weather	which	heard
where	whether	witch	herd

A. Use spelling words to complete the story.

The cowboys on the range watched the sky to see what the

_____ might do. They had _____ that rain and wind

were coming in from the north.

They decided to drive the _____ to a safer part of the ranch

to wait out the storm.

B. Find the missing letters. Then write the word.

1. ___ h ___ ___ ___ ___ ___   _____

2. ___ ___ i ___ ___   _____

3. ___ ___ t ___ ___   _____

4. ___ ___ e ___ ___   _____

C. Use each spelling word in a sentence.

heard _____

which _____

weather _____

herd _____

whether _____

wear _____

where _____

witch _____

Words with *ph*

phrase	geography	photo	elephant
telephone	sphere	alphabet	nephew

A. Fill in each blank with a spelling word.

1. I learned the names of countries in my _____ class.

2. My cousin knows the letters of the Greek _____.

3. "Better late than never" is a _____ I often hear.

4. She has a _____ of her family on the wall.

5. The _____ sprayed water from its trunk.

6. The _____ rang three times before I answered it.

7. Something round like a ball is called a _____.

8. My _____ is my brother's son.

B. Divide each spelling word into syllables on the lines below.

1. telephone ____ ___ _____   2. alphabet ___ ____ ____

3. elephant ____ ___ _____   4. photo ____ ___

5. geography ___ __ ____ __   6. sphere _____

7. phrase _____   8. nephew ____ ___

C. Write a spelling word under each picture.

1. _____   2. _____   3. _____

Name _____

Words with *ph*

phrase	geography	photo	elephant
telephone	sphere	alphabet	nephew

A. **Write the correct spelling word beside each clue.**

_____ 1. the study of Earth and its features

_____ 2. a round object

_____ 3. a short word for "photograph"

_____ 4. an instrument that carries voice signals from one place to another

_____ 5. a group of words

_____ 6. the letters of a language

_____ 7. the son of one's brother or sister

_____ 8. a very large animal with a trunk

B. **Use each spelling word in a sentence.**

photo _____

nephew _____

elephant _____

geography _____

telephone _____

alphabet _____

phrase _____

sphere _____

C. **All of the spelling words contain the letters *ph*. What consonant do these letters sound like?** _____

50

LESSON 13

Words with *ph*

phrase	geography	photo	elephant
telephone	sphere	alphabet	nephew

A. Write each word three times.

geography _____ _____ _____

elephant _____ _____ _____

alphabet _____ _____ _____

phrase _____ _____ _____

nephew _____ _____ _____

sphere _____ _____ _____

photo _____ _____ _____

telephone _____ _____ _____

B. Complete these exercises with spelling words.

1. Which word has the most syllables? _____

2. Which words contain two *e*'s?

_____ _____ _____

C. Use spelling words to complete the story.

My _____ likes to write short stories. Last month, he sent

one of them to a magazine. This week, he got a _____ call

from a woman who works for the magazine. She liked my nephew's story.

They want to print it in five or six months.

They'll take a _____ of him to go with the story. My

nephew is excited. Now he feels like a real writer!

Name _____

Words with *ph*

| phrase | geography | photo | elephant |
| telephone | sphere | alphabet | nephew |

A. Write the spelling words in alphabetical order.

1. _____ 2. _____ 3. _____

4. _____ 5. _____ 6. _____

7. _____ 8. _____

B. Put an *X* on the word that is <u>not</u> the same.

1. phrase	phrase	phraes	phrase	phrase
2. telephone	telephone	telephone	telephone	telehpone
3. alphabet	alphabat	alphabet	alphabet	alphabet
4. sphere	sphere	shpere	sphere	sphere
5. geography	geagraphy	geography	geography	geography
6. nephew	nephew	nepheu	nephew	nephew

C. One word is wrong in each sentence. Circle the wrong word. Then fill in the blank with a spelling word that makes sense.

1. In Africa, we rode a huge ant.   _____

2. My brother's son is my ear.   _____

3. Would someone please answer the carrot?   _____

4. I took a broom with my new camera.   _____

5. The soup had noodles shaped like the bathtub. _____

6. We learn about Earth in oatmeal class.   _____

LESSON 14

Comparative words

smaller	smarter	thicker	cheaper
fresher	quicker	stronger	older

A. Fill in each blank with a spelling word.

1. If I study a lot, I'll get _____.

2. A hill is _____ than a mountain.

3. This fish smells _____ than that one.

4. Eggs are _____ by the dozen.

5. It is _____ to go by airplane than by bus.

6. She can lift more, because her arms are _____.

7. My friend is three days _____ than I am.

8. If we add more ice cream, our milkshake will be _____.

B. Match each spelling word with its antonym.

_____ 1. smaller   **a.** younger

_____ 2. quicker   **b.** thinner

_____ 3. thicker   **c.** weaker

_____ 4. older   **d.** larger

_____ 5. stronger   **e.** slower

_____ 6. cheaper   **f.** more stale

_____ 7. fresher   **g.** more expensive

C. Answer the question.

Which spelling words rhyme with each other?

_____ _____

Name _____

LESSON 14   Comparative words

smaller	smarter	thicker	cheaper
fresher	quicker	stronger	older

A. Write the root word of each spelling word.

1. smaller _____   **2.** smarter _____

3. thicker _____   **4.** cheaper _____

5. fresher _____   **6.** quicker _____

7. stronger _____   **8.** older _____

B. Put an *X* on the word that is <u>not</u> the same.

1. thicker	tricker	thicker	thicker	thicker
2. quicker	quicker	quicker	quicken	quicker
3. fresher	fresher	flesher	fresher	fresher
4. smarter	smarter	smarter	smarter	smarten

C. Complete these exercises.

1. Which spelling word begins with a vowel? _____

2. Which spelling words begin with *sm*?

_____   _____

3. Circle the one vowel that is in all the spelling words.

    a   e   i   o   u

4. Which spelling word has the most letters? _____

5. All of the spelling words have _____ syllables.

                     (one, two)

54

LESSON 14

Comparative words

smaller	**smarter**	**thicker**	**cheaper**
fresher	**quicker**	**stronger**	**older**

A. Match each root word with its synonym.

______	1. smart	a. fast
______	2. old	b. powerful
______	3. strong	c. little
______	4. quick	d. wise
______	5. small	e. elderly
______	6. cheap	f. wide
______	7. thick	g. inexpensive

B. Circle the word that is the same as the top one.

smaller	quicker	fresher	stronger	cheaper	older
smeller	quicker	frasher	stranger	chaeper	older
snaller	quacker	fresker	stronger	cheapen	odler
smaller	qnicker	frehser	stringer	cheaber	olden
smallen	quieter	fresher	stonger	cheaper	oldre

C. Use spelling words to complete the story.

I knew a boy who grew up with six ______________ brothers. The brothers teased the boy for being ______________ than they were. The boy decided to work hard to become ___________ than his brothers. When the brothers saw how strong he was and how hard he worked, they admired him and never teased him again.

Name ______________________________________

Comparative words

smaller	smarter	thicker	cheaper
fresher	quicker	stronger	older

A. Find the missing letters. Then write the word.

1. __ r __ __ __ __ __   _____

2. __ __ __ __ l __ __   _____

3. __ __ r __ __ __ __ __   _____

B. Find the hidden words on the list.

smaller	smarter	thicker	cheaper	wear
fresher	quicker	stronger	older	whole
phrase	geography	photo	elephant	scrubbed
telephone	sphere	alphabet	nephew	herd

```
r  a  o  a  l  p  h  a  b  e  t  e  a  s  e
t  e  a  p  a  n  g  e  s  a  e  a  c  c  a
h  s  p  h  e  r  e  t  m  c  l  t  e  h  s
i  m  r  o  l  i  o  s  a  n  e  p  h  e  w
c  a  i  t  e  t  g  s  l  h  p  i  e  a  s
k  r  s  o  p  s  r  t  l  m  h  n  r  p  c
e  t  t  p  h  p  a  r  e  o  o  l  d  e  r
r  e  w  e  a  r  p  o  r  n  n  g  q  r  u
o  r  h  n  n  p  h  r  a  s  e  b  u  t  b
m  t  o  i  t  r  y  n  r  k  n  a  i  w  b
s  s  l  n  h  e  t  g  t  h  a  n  c  o  e
a  f  e  s  t  r  o  n  g  e  r  e  k  t  d
n  r  f  g  c  n  s  e  h  r  s  e  e  h  n
t  f  r  e  s  h  e  r  a  d  o  a  r  r  e
```

LESSON 15

Superlative words

softest	cleanest	quickest	brightest
warmest	neatest	sharpest	poorest

A. Fill in each blank with a spelling word.

1. Which pencil has the _____ point?

2. This soap gets your hands the _____.

3. The _____ bulb we have is one hundred watts.

4. Your notebook is always the _____.

5. That was the _____ I've ever done in a race.

6. Last summer was the _____ that I can remember.

7. Our skin is _____ when we're babies.

8. Ten minutes is my _____ time for running one mile.

B. Write the correct spelling word beside each clue.

_____ 1. able to cut the best

_____ 2. having the least money, or worst

_____ 3. having the most light or color

_____ 4. cleanest

_____ 5. fastest

_____ 6. least hard

C. Write the spelling words in alphabetical order.

1. _____   2. _____   3. _____

4. _____   5. _____   6. _____

7. _____   8. _____

Name _____

57

LESSON 15

Superlative words

softest	cleanest	quickest	brightest
warmest	neatest	sharpest	poorest

A. Write the root word of each spelling word.

1. softest _____   2. cleanest _____

3. quickest _____   4. brightest _____

5. warmest _____   6. neatest _____

7. sharpest _____   8. poorest _____

B. Use each root word in a sentence.

quick _____

bright _____

clean _____

neat _____

poor _____

warm _____

soft _____

sharp _____

C. Circle the word that is the same as the top one.

softest	sharpest	warmest	quickest	neatest	poorest
soffest	sherpast	warmest	quickest	neetest	poorest
softset	sharpast	wramest	quickect	naetest	porest
softest	sharpasf	wamrest	guickest	neatest	pourest
softcst	sharpest	wermest	quickeet	neafest	poorets

Superlative words

| softest | cleanest | quickest | brightest |
| warmest | neatest | sharpest | poorest |

A. Find the missing letters. Then write the word.

1. ___ l ___ ___ ___ ___ ___ ___   _____

2. ___ ___ ___ g ___ ___ ___ ___ ___   _____

3. ___ ___ f ___ ___ ___ ___   _____

4. ___ h ___ ___ ___ ___ ___ ___   _____

B. Divide each spelling word into syllables on the lines below.

1. softest _____ _____   2. cleanest _____ _____

3. quickest _____ _____   4. brightest _____ _____

5. warmest _____ _____   6. neatest _____ _____

7. sharpest _____ _____   8. poorest _____ _____

C. Use spelling words to complete the story.

Tuesday was my birthday. I waited all day, but by the afternoon no one had wished me a happy birthday. I felt pretty bad. At soccer practice, I couldn't do anything right. It was the _____ I'd ever done. I walked home sadly.

When I opened the front door, all my friends yelled "Surprise!" It was a party! They hadn't forgotten my birthday after all. They gave me a new tent and sleeping bag. The tent was the _____ orange color! The sleeping bag was made of down and was the _____ one I'd ever felt. What a good day Tuesday turned out to be.

Name _____

Superlative words

softest	cleanest	quickest	brightest
warmest	neatest	sharpest	poorest

A. Match each spelling word with its antonym.

_____ 1. softest   **a.** dullest

_____ 2. warmest   **b.** darkest

_____ 3. cleanest   **c.** richest

_____ 4. quickest   **d.** hardest

_____ 5. sharpest   **e.** coolest

_____ 6. brightest   **f.** dirtiest

_____ 7. poorest   **g.** slowest

B. Put an X on the word that is not the same.

1. softest	softest	softest	sotfest	softest
2. warmest	warmest	warnest	warmest	warmest
3. cleanest	cleanest	cleanest	cleanest	claenest
4. neatest	neatest	neatset	neatest	neatest
5. quickest	guickest	quickest	quickest	quickest
6. brightest	brightest	brightest	brigthest	brightest
7. sharpest	sharpest	sharpest	scharpest	sharpest
8. poorest	poorert	poorest	poorest	poorest

C. Which spelling words have a long e sound?

_____ _____

Words with -er

clever	chapter	silver	wander
whisper	cover	corner	enter

A. Fill in each blank with a spelling word.

1. _____ One in our history book is about the Civil War.

2. Have you ever seen a _____ dollar?

3. We can _____ through this door.

4. Her voice is so soft, it's almost a _____.

5. Don't _____ too far, or you may get lost.

6. What a _____ invention that is!

7. The _____ on a book protects the pages.

8. Wait for me at the _____ of the street.

B. Write a spelling word under each picture.

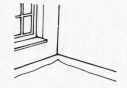

1. _____ 2. _____ 3. _____

C. Find the missing letters. Then write the word.

1. ___ ___ ___ p ___ ___ ___   _____

2. ___ ___ r ___ ___ ___   _____

3. ___ ___ v ___ ___   _____

4. w ___ ___ ___ ___ ___   _____

Name _____

LESSON 16

Words with -er

clever	chapter	silver	wander
whisper	cover	corner	enter

A. Divide each spelling word into syllables on the lines below.

1. clever _____ _____
2. chapter _____ _____
3. cover _____ _____
4. corner _____ _____
5. silver _____ _____
6. whisper _____ _____
7. wander _____ _____
8. enter _____ _____

B. Match each spelling word with its antonym.

_____ 1. enter   a. expose

_____ 2. clever   b. shout

_____ 3. cover   c. exit

_____ 4. whisper   d. settle

_____ 5. wander   e. dull

C. Complete these exercises.

1. Circle the vowel that is <u>not</u> found in the spelling words.

      a   e   i   o   u

2. Which spelling word begins with a vowel? _____

3. Which spelling words end with *ver*?

   _____   _____   _____

D. Finish the sentence.

I would like to <u>wander</u> _____.

LESSON 16

Words with *-er*

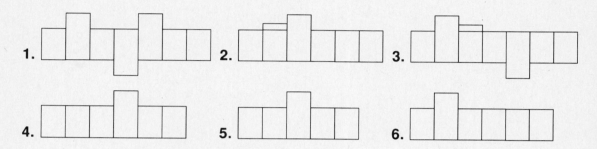

clever	chapter	silver	wander
whisper	cover	corner	enter

A. Fill in the boxes with the right words.

1.

2.

3.

4.

5.

6.

B. Use spelling words to complete the story.

My niece had to study for a spelling test last night. The test covered the last _____ of her book. She has done well on all the other spelling tests. She always gets the highest grades in her class.

My niece asked the rest of us to _____, so we wouldn't disturb her. I sat quietly across the room and watched her study.

My niece looked at the words for a while. Then she said them out loud. After that, she shut the book's _____ and wrote down the words. She took her time. If a word looked wrong, she thought for a while, then changed a letter or two. I could see that she was working very hard.

After she had written all the words, she checked her spelling. She remembered them all correctly.

On the test the next day, my niece got all of the words right. She was proud, and so were her parents. Next year, she'll _____ the second grade.

Name _____

Words with *-er*

clever	chapter	silver	wander
whisper	cover	corner	enter

A. Match each spelling word with the right clue.

_____ **1.** cover   **a.** skillful

_____ **2.** wander   **b.** go in

_____ **3.** clever   **c.** angle

_____ **4.** enter   **d.** murmur

_____ **5.** whisper   **e.** roam

_____ **6.** corner   **f.** blanket

B. Use each spelling word in a sentence.

whisper _____

silver _____

wander _____

chapter _____

clever _____

cover _____

corner _____

enter _____

C. Write words that begin like each word below.

whisper   chapter   wander

_____   _____   _____

_____   _____   _____

LESSON 17   Homonyms

pour	won	deer	meat
pore	one	dear	meet

A. Fill in each blank with a spelling word.

1. Will you _____ me a glass of milk?

2. My friend _____ the race by six seconds.

3. There is a _____ standing in the road.

4. I will _____ you at noon.

5. What a _____ friend you are!

6. Seven is _____ more than six.

7. He likes to _____ over old maps for hours.

8. Beef is _____ from cattle.

B. Fill in the boxes with the right words.

1.

2.

3.

4.

C. Write the correct spelling word beside its antonym.

1. lost _____   2. sprinkle _____

3. many _____   4. avoid _____

D. Reverse the letters of each word below to find a spelling word.

1. now _____   2. teem _____

Name _____

Homonyms

pour	won	deer	meat
pore	one	dear	meet

A. Write the correct spelling word beside each clue.

_____ **1.** to get together, or to be introduced to

_____ **2.** a single item

_____ **3.** a small opening in the skin, or to study very carefully

_____ **4.** to make something flow freely, or a heavy fall of rain

_____ **5.** the past tense of "win"

_____ **6.** well loved, or expensive

_____ **7.** a hoofed mammal

B. Use the spelling words in sentences. If the word has two meanings, as shown above, write a sentence for each meaning.

meet _____

_____

deer _____

won _____

pore _____

_____

meat _____

dear _____

_____

one _____

Homonyms

| pour | won | deer | meat |
| pore | one | dear | meet |

A. Use spelling words to complete the story.

This is my first year on the track team at school. We practice every afternoon. _____ of my teammates is so good that he seems to fly when he does the high jump.

A girl on the team is a champion runner. She has _____ all her races this year.

I get nervous before each _____. But when I'm running, I feel great. I like to do my best and to hear the crowds cheer me on.

B. Put an *X* on the word that is <u>not</u> the same.

1. pore	pore	poer	pore	pore
2. won	now	won	won	won
3. dear	dear	dear	dear	deer
4. meet	meet	meet	mete	meet
5. pour	poun	pour	pour	pour
6. deer	deer	derr	deer	deer
7. meat	meat	mate	meat	meat
8. one	one	ome	one	one

C. Write the spelling words in alphabetical order.

1. _____   2. _____   3. _____   4. _____

5. _____   6. _____   7. _____   8. _____

Name _____

Homonyms

pour	won	deer	meat
pore	one	dear	meet

A. Below are pairs of guide words. Write the spelling word that would come between each pair in the dictionary.

meat **1.** mean—mechanic

_____ **2.** day—decode

_____ **3.** poppy—pose

_____ **4.** under—wring

_____ **5.** on—only

_____ **6.** medal—met

_____ **7.** pound—pout

_____ **8.** debate—deface

B. Match each spelling word with the right clue.

_____ **1.** dear   **a.** hamburger and turkey, for example

_____ **2.** one   **b.** to join another person or persons

_____ **3.** pore   **c.** the way to put milk on cereal

_____ **4.** meat   **d.** precious, worth much, or cared for

_____ **5.** pour   **e.** the number of suns our planet has

_____ **6.** meet   **f.** to look intently

_____ **7.** deer   **g.** an animal that sometimes has antlers

C. Words that sound the same but have different spellings and meanings are called _____.

Words with *-ue*

rescue	statue	argue	glue
avenue	true	continue	clue

A. Fill in each blank with a spelling word.

1. A fact is a _____ statement.

2. I can't guess the answer without a _____.

3. The _____ was made of carved stone.

4. The daring _____ saved ten lives.

5. Our city planted palms along the _____.

6. Why do some sisters and brothers _____?

7. Let's _____ the game after lunch.

8. Use _____ to hold the sticks together.

B. Write the correct spelling word beside its antonym.

1. false _____ 2. agree _____

3. quit _____ 4. endanger _____

C. Write words that begin like each word below.

statue	true	glue	clue
_____	_____	_____	_____
_____	_____	_____	_____
_____	_____	_____	_____
_____	_____	_____	_____
_____	_____	_____	_____

Name _____

Words with *-ue*

rescue	statue	argue	glue
avenue	true	continue	clue

A. Write the spelling words in alphabetical order.

1. _____ 2. _____ 3. _____ 4. _____

5. _____ 6. _____ 7. _____ 8. _____

B. Write the correct spelling word beside its synonym.

1. debate _____ 2. save _____

3. monument _____ 4. persist _____

5. hint _____ 6. accurate _____

C. Write each word three times.

rescue _____ _____ _____

avenue _____ _____ _____

argue _____ _____ _____

statue _____ _____ _____

continue _____ _____ _____

glue _____ _____ _____

D. Put an *X* on the word that is <u>not</u> the same.

1. glue	glue	glue	clue	glue
2. avenue	awenue	avenue	avenue	avenue
3. rescue	rescue	rescue	rescue	recue
4. true	true	true	true	treu

LESSON 18   # Words with *-ue*

rescue	statue	argue	glue
avenue	true	continue	clue

A. Circle the word that is the same as the top one.

rescue	avenue	statue	argue	glue	continue
recseu	averue	slatue	angue	gleu	contniue
resceu	aveune	statue	argae	glue	contineu
rescue	avneue	satue	argue	gule	continue
nescue	avenue	stateu	agrue	geul	cnotinue
reccue	awenue	statute	arigue	gloo	confinue

B. Finish the sentences.

1. It is <u>true</u> that _____.

2. People shouldn't <u>argue</u> about _____.

C. Use spelling words to complete the story.

Our town has many visitors from other countries. Each day you see them walking around the town square and taking pictures by the river.

There are fine old buildings to see in our town. And we have a beautiful _____ that is our main street. There are tall elm trees lining it. In a square near the avenue, there's a huge _____ of our town's first mayor. There are all sorts of tours you can take on foot or by bus.

I like to talk to the tourists. Many of them speak our language. It's fun to learn about their lives. I hope these people will _____ to come to our town.

Name _____

71

Words with *-ue*

rescue	statue	argue	glue
avenue	true	continue	clue

A. Fill in the boxes with the right words.

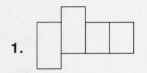

1.

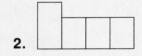

2.

3.

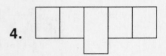

4.

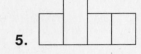

5.

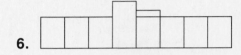

6.

B. Count the number of syllables in each spelling word. Write each word under the correct number of syllables.

1	2	3
_____	_____	_____
_____	_____	_____
_____	_____	

C. Write a paragraph using two of the spelling words.

_____

_____

_____

_____

_____

_____

_____

Words with *-al*

trial	metal	dial	formal
normal	personal	pedal	editorial

A. Fill in each blank with a spelling word.

1. When you have a fever, your temperature is above _____.

2. Silver is a type of _____.

3. Did you read the _____ in the newspaper?

4. The movie star gave the reporter a _____ interview.

5. A dinner with the king is always _____.

6. Will you _____ my telephone number, please?

7. We saw a _____ at the courthouse today.

8. I need to buy a new _____ for my bicycle.

B. Write the correct spelling word beside its synonym.

1. opinion _____   2. regular _____

3. private _____   4. proper _____

C. Write the spelling words in alphabetical order.

1. _____   2. _____   3. _____

4. _____   5. _____   6. _____

7. _____   8. _____

D. Below are pairs of guide words. Write the spelling word that would come between each pair in the dictionary.

_____ 1. peal—pen

_____ 2. dear—door

Name _____

LESSON 19

Words with -al

trial	metal	dial	formal
normal	personal	pedal	editorial

A. Use spelling words to complete the story.

Last night we had a bad storm. The lights went out for a while, and the telephones wouldn't work. When I would _____ a number, all I got was silence.

There were great flashes of lightning and crashing thunder. We have a lightning rod made of _____. It protects the house if lightning strikes it.

We could tell that a storm was coming. The clouds didn't look

_____ all day, and our animals were acting strange.

B. Fill in the boxes with the right words.

1. 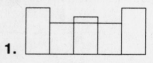   2.    3.

4. 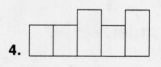   5.    6.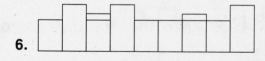

C. Write the correct spelling word beside its antonym.

1. casual _____   2. unusual _____

D. The words "pedal" and "peddle" are homonyms. Use each word correctly in a sentence.

pedal _____

peddle _____

74

LESSON 19

Words with *-al*

trial	metal	dial	formal
normal	personal	pedal	editorial

A. Divide each spelling word into syllables on the lines below.

1. trial _____ ____   **2.** normal _____ _____

3. metal _____ ____   **4.** personal _____ _____ ____

5. dial ____ ____   **6.** pedal _____ ____

7. formal _____ _____   **8.** editorial ___ __ ___ ___ ___

B. Write a paragraph using two of the spelling words.

_____

_____

_____

_____

_____

_____

_____

_____

_____

_____

C. Find the missing letters. Then write the word.

1. f ___ ___ ___ ___ ___   _____

2. ___ ___ r ___ ___ ___ ___ ___   _____

3. ___ ___ d ___ ___   _____

4. n ___ ___ ___ ___ ___   _____

Name _____

Words with *-al*

trial	metal	dial	formal
normal	personal	pedal	editorial

A. Match each spelling word with the right clue.

_____ **1.** metal   **a.** opinion written in a newspaper

_____ **2.** normal   **b.** something that is private

_____ **3.** editorial   **c.** what coins are made of

_____ **4.** trial   **d.** not unusual

_____ **5.** personal   **e.** what a person accused of a crime has a right to

B. Write a spelling word under each picture.

1. _____ 2. _____ 3. _____

C. Use each spelling word in a sentence.

pedal _____

personal _____

trial _____

formal _____

dial _____

normal _____

metal _____

Words with *-el*

cruel	towel	fuel	barrel
jewel	duel	bushel	vowel

A. Fill in each blank with a spelling word.

1. The letter *a* is a _____.

2. I picked a _____ of tomatoes.

3. After a bath, I dry off with a _____.

4. A _____ of oil equals forty-two gallons.

5. Gas is a _____ that is used in cars.

6. The _____ in the ring shines in the light.

7. The play was about a king who was _____.

8. A _____ is a type of fight between two people.

B. Circle the word that is the same as the top one.

<u>cruel</u>	<u>towel</u>	<u>fuel</u>	<u>bushel</u>	<u>barrel</u>	<u>vowel</u>
curel	towle	fule	bushel	barrle	vowle
creul	towel	flue	bushal	bannel	vouel
cruel	touel	feul	bushle	barnel	vowel
crule	twoel	fuel	buhsel	barrel	vomel

C. Write the four spelling words that rhyme with each other.

_____ _____ _____ _____

D. Below is a pair of guide words. Write the spelling word that would come between the pair in the dictionary.

_____ jet—jewelry

Name _____

Words with -el

cruel	towel	fuel	barrel
jewel	duel	bushel	vowel

A. Use spelling words to complete the story.

My sister likes to wash her hair in rainwater. She thinks it makes her

hair look better. She bought a big, wooden _____ to catch the rain

in. It sits on the side of the house. Twice a week, my sister grabs her

shampoo and a _____ and goes outside to wash her hair. She dips

rainwater from the barrel to wet and rinse her hair.

One day, I put my pet frog in the rain barrel. My sister saw the frog and

screamed. She said it was a _____ joke to play on her.

B. Write the correct spelling word beside each clue.

_____ 1. a container for fruits and vegetables, or a unit of dry measure

_____ 2. a kind of speech sound

_____ 3. a contest between two people

_____ 4. a container, often with a wide middle

_____ 5. something that makes heat or power

_____ 6. a stone or a gem

C. The words "dual" and "duel" are homonyms. Use each word correctly in a sentence.

dual _____

duel _____

Words with *-el*

cruel	towel	fuel	barrel
jewel	duel	bushel	vowel

A. Write the spelling words that contain *ow*.

_____   _____

B. Find the hidden words on the list.

cruel	towel	fuel	barrel	continue
morsel	duel	bushel	vowel	chopper
trial	metal	dial	formal	enter
normal	personal	pedal	editorial	clue

```
c  h  o  p  p  e  r  s  o  y  c  o  b  r
o  a  e  d  f  u  e  l  u  t  r  i  a  l
n  a  r  t  o  p  d  y  r  o  u  v  r  p
t  t  a  q  r  r  i  a  c  w  e  i  r  e
i  o  t  o  m  e  t  a  l  e  l  d  e  d
n  b  s  i  a  v  o  w  e  l  t  n  l  a
u  u  r  m  l  e  r  d  l  a  c  o  j  l
e  r  i  o  m  d  i  a  l  u  r  r  e  l
o  f  a  r  c  h  a  d  a  g  c  m  s  c
n  b  u  s  h  e  l  y  u  h  l  a  m  s
s  a  p  e  r  s  o  n  a  l  u  l  i  t
d  u  e  l  e  s  d  e  n  t  e  r  f  o
```

C. Write the correct spelling word beside its antonym.

1. consonant _____   2. kind _____

Name _____

Words with -el

cruel	towel	fuel	barrel
jewel	duel	bushel	vowel

A. Write the spelling words in alphabetical order.

1. _____ 2. _____ 3. _____ 4. _____

5. _____ 6. _____ 7. _____ 8. _____

B. Write a spelling word under each picture.

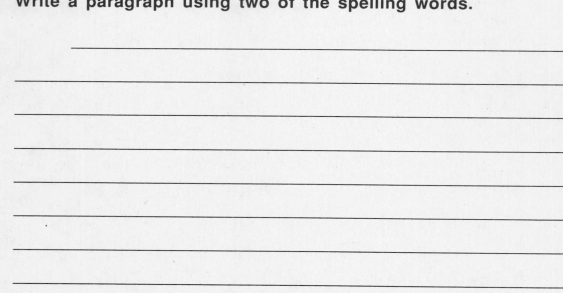

1. _____ 2. _____ 3. _____

C. Write a paragraph using two of the spelling words.

_____

_____

_____

_____

_____

_____

_____

_____

D. Find the missing letters. Then write the word.

1. __ __ s h __ __   _____

2. __ r __ __ __   _____

LESSON 21   # Words with *-le*

staple	maple	purple	simple
apple	people	steeple	cable

A. Fill in each blank with a spelling word.

1. Many _____ need eight hours of sleep each night.

2. Building a house is not a _____ task.

3. Do you have _____ TV?

4. I can see the church _____ from all parts of town.

5. Let's make an _____ pie.

6. Vermont is known for its _____ syrup.

7. Please _____ these papers together.

8. _____ paint can be made by mixing red and blue paint.

B. Write the spelling words in alphabetical order.

1. _____   2. _____   3. _____   4. _____

5. _____   6. _____   7. _____   8. _____

C. Divide each spelling word into syllables on the lines below.

1. staple _____ _____   2. apple _____ _____

3. maple _____ _____   4. people _____ _____

5. purple _____ _____   6. steeple _____ _____

7. simple _____ _____   8. cable _____ _____

D. Write the correct spelling word beside its synonym.

1. easy _____   2. persons _____

Name _____

81

LESSON 21

Words with *-le*

staple	maple	purple	simple
apple	people	steeple	cable

A. Circle the vowels that are in the spelling words.

a   e   i   o   u

B. Below are pairs of guide words. Write the spelling word that would come between each pair in the dictionary.

_____ **1.** steam—stone

_____ **2.** stamp—steal

_____ **3.** shower—sleep

_____ **4.** cab—cattle

_____ **5.** pinch—puzzle

_____ **6.** among—art

_____ **7.** ship—sin

C. Write a paragraph using two of the spelling words.

_____

_____

_____

_____

_____

_____

_____

_____

Words with *-le*

staple	maple	purple	simple
apple	people	steeple	cable

A. Put an *X* on the word that is <u>not</u> the same.

1. staple	staple	staple	staple	stable
2. apple	apple	apple	appel	apple
3. maple	mable	maple	maple	maple
4. people	people	poeple	people	people
5. purple	purple	purple	perple	purple
6. steeple	steeble	steeple	steeple	steeple

B. Complete these exercises with spelling words.

1. Which word contains three *e*'s? _____

2. Which words contain two *p*'s?

_____   _____   _____

C. Write each word three times.

apple   _____   _____   _____

simple   _____   _____   _____

staple   _____   _____   _____

maple   _____   _____   _____

people   _____   _____   _____

steeple   _____   _____   _____

cable   _____   _____   _____

Name _____

Words with *-le*

staple	maple	purple	simple
apple	people	steeple	cable

A. Write the correct spelling word beside each clue.

_____ **1.** a church tower

_____ **2.** a piece of metal pushed through paper

_____ **3.** easy to do or understand

_____ **4.** a fruit that grows on trees

_____ **5.** a type of tree

B. Use each spelling word in a sentence.

people _____

purple _____

cable _____

steeple _____

simple _____

apple _____

C. Use spelling words to complete the story.

I know a woman who makes beautiful kites. One day she made a big

_____ kite with a tail like a dragon. We went with her to the

soccer field to try it out. She soon had the kite flying high above us.

A crowd of _____ gathered to watch the kite dip and wave in

the sky.

LESSON 22

Words with *-dle*

cradle	middle	poodle	handle
needle	peddle	riddle	saddle

A. Fill in each blank with a spelling word.

1. Do you know the answer to this _____?

2. I bought a new _____ for my horse.

3. The letter *m* is in the _____ of the alphabet.

4. It's not always easy to thread a _____.

5. The baby is sleeping in her _____.

6. To sell goods from place to place is to _____.

7. A _____ is a dog with curly hair.

8. Can this broken door _____ be fixed?

B. Fill in the boxes with the right words.

1. 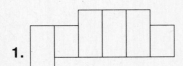   2. 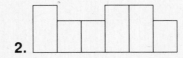   3.

C. Write the correct spelling word beside its synonym.

1. center _____   2. puzzle _____

3. bed _____   4. pin _____

5. sell _____

D. Write the spelling words that rhyme with each other.

_____   _____

Name _____

85

LESSON 22

Words with -dle

| cradle | middle | poodle | handle |
| needle | peddle | riddle | saddle |

A. Write a spelling word under each picture.

1. _____   2. _____   3. _____

4. _____   5. _____   6. _____

B. Circle the word that is the same as the top one.

cradle	peddle	middle	poodle	handle	saddle
crable	pebble	middel	poodle	hardel	sabble
crabel	pebbel	mideld	qoodel	handel	saddle
cnadle	peddle	mibble	pooble	handle	sadle
cradle	pedle	middle	poole	hanedl	sable

C. Divide each spelling word into syllables on the lines below.

1. cradle _____ _____   2. needle _____ _____

3. middle _____ _____   4. riddle _____ _____

5. handle _____ _____   6. saddle _____ _____

7. peddle _____ _____   8. poodle _____ _____

86

Words with -dle

cradle	middle	poodle	handle
needle	peddle	riddle	saddle

A. Write the correct spelling word beside each clue.

_____ 1. a puzzling question, or to make many holes in

_____ 2. a breed of dog with curly hair

_____ 3. a metal object used for sewing, or to tease

_____ 4. a baby's bed, or to hold carefully in your hands or arms

_____ 5. the center

_____ 6. to travel about selling goods

B. Write a paragraph using two of the spelling words.

_____

_____

_____

_____

_____

_____

_____

_____

_____

C. Finish the sentences.

1. I know a <u>riddle</u> about _____.

2. You can use a <u>needle</u> to _____.

Name _____

Words with *-dle*

cradle	middle	poodle	handle
needle	peddle	riddle	saddle

A. Find the missing letters. Then write the word.

1. ___ ___ e ___ ___ ___   _____

2. ___ ___ o ___ ___ ___   _____

3. s ___ ___ ___ ___ ___   _____

4. ___ r ___ ___ ___ ___   _____

B. Use spelling words to complete the story.

Last week, a circus came to town. We watched the men put up the tents. Then we went inside to see the performers practice for the show. Instead of costumes, they were wearing regular clothes. We met a man who knows how to _____ snakes. Then we saw a woman riding a horse with no _____. The woman stood on the horse's back, as he trotted around the _____ of the ring. I liked watching the circus people do amazing tricks in ordinary, everyday clothes.

C. Below are pairs of guide words. Write the spelling word that would come between each pair in the dictionary.

_____ 1. neat—nest

_____ 2. card—crazy

_____ 3. sad—sudden

_____ 4. pear—pest

_____ 5. hamster—hang

Homonyms

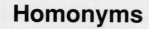

pain	wood	led	break
pane	would	lead	brake

A. Fill in each blank with a spelling word.

1. _____ you like to walk by the lake?

2. When the day was done, we _____ the horses to the barn.

3. I saw him _____ the home run record.

4. The hand _____ keeps the car from rolling.

5. Pencil _____ is made of graphite.

6. Do you have a stove that burns _____?

7. She threw the rock through the window _____.

8. I get a _____ in my side when I run too hard.

B. Circle the word that is the same as the top one.

pain	would	lead	pane	break	brake
paim	woulb	lead	pare	braek	break
pair	wuold	leed	pane	brake	brake
pain	woold	leab	pain	break	breke
pane	would	lede	panc	breek	brakc

C. Write the correct spelling word beside its synonym.

1. ache _____   2. lumber _____

D. Write the spelling words in alphabetical order.

1. _____ 2. _____ 3. _____ 4. _____

5. _____ 6. _____ 7. _____ 8. _____

Name _____

89

Homonyms

pain	wood	led	break
pane	would	lead	brake

A. Use spelling words to complete the story.

I was playing a game of baseball in my neighborhood this morning. The score was tied. It was my turn at bat. I picked up my lucky bat made of _____. After a couple of practice swings, I stepped up to the plate.

I wanted to get a home run, to _____ the tie and win the game for my team. The pitcher threw the ball. I swung and hit it. Crack! The ball zoomed far out past the field, over the fence, and right through a neighbor's window. I heard the _____ of glass shatter. At that moment, I didn't care about the home run. I just wanted to run home.

B. Write a paragraph using two of the spelling words.

_____

_____

_____

_____

_____

_____

C. Write the spelling words that rhyme with the words below.

1. rain   gain   _____

2. good   hood   _____

3. bed   said   _____

LESSON 23

Homonyms

pain	wood	led	break
pane	would	lead	brake

A. Write the correct spelling word beside each clue.

_____ **1.** a metal used to make pipe

_____ **2.** an unpleasant feeling

_____ **3.** a sheet of glass in a window

_____ **4.** the opposite of "wouldn't"

_____ **5.** the hard material under the bark of trees

_____ **6.** guided

_____ **7.** to smash, or a short rest period

_____ **8.** to come to a stop, or a thing used to make something stop

B. Use each spelling word in a sentence.

would _____

pane _____

led _____

brake _____

pain _____

lead _____

break _____

C. Fill in the boxes with the right words.

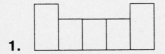 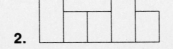 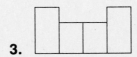

1.   **2.**   **3.**

Name _____

Homonyms

pain	wood	led	break
pane	would	lead	brake

A. Write the correct spelling word beside its antonym.

1. repair _____   2. followed _____

B. Below are pairs of guide words. Write the spelling word that would come between each pair in the dictionary.

_____ 1. page—panda

_____ 2. lazy—leave

_____ 3. brave—breathe

_____ 4. won—word

C. Put an X on the word that is <u>not</u> the same.

1. pain	pain	pain	pair	pain
2. wood	wood	wood	wood	woob
3. lead	lead	laed	lead	lead
4. break	braek	break	break	break
5. pane	pane	pane	pane	pine
6. would	woold	would	would	would

D. Find the missing letters. Then write the word.

1. ___ ___ i ___   _____

2. ___ ___ n ___   _____

3. l ___ ___ ___   _____

Words with *-tle*

beetle	tattle	title	battle
gentle	kettle	settle	rattle

A. Fill in each blank with a spelling word.

1. I boiled the water in a _____.

2. Our dog is very _____ with children.

3. *Target: Spelling* is the _____ of this book.

4. Which snake has a tail that can _____?

5. A _____ has four wings.

6. I hope to _____ here for a few years.

7. The _____ was won, but the war was lost.

8. To _____ is to tell on someone.

B. Put an *X* on the word that is <u>not</u> the same.

1. beetle	battle	beetle	beetle	beetle
2. would	would	would	would	world
3. gentle	gentle	gentle	gertle	gentle
4. break	break	breck	break	break

C. Find the missing letters. Then write the word.

1. k ___ ___ ___ ___ ___   _____

2. b e ___ ___ ___ ___   _____

3. ___ ___ n ___ ___ ___   _____

4. t ___ ___ ___ ___ ___   _____

Name _____

Words with -tle

beetle	tattle	title	battle
gentle	kettle	settle	rattle

A. Circle the word that is the same as the top one.

gentle	title	kettle	settle	rattle	battle
gentle	tilte	dettel	setle	ratle	battel
gertle	titel	kattle	settle	rettle	batel
gentel	tietl	kettle	settel	rattle	batle
genetl	title	ketle	setel	ratel	battle

B. Write the spelling words in alphabetical order.

1. _____ 2. _____ 3. _____ 4. _____

5. _____ 6. _____ 7. _____ 8. _____

C. Use spelling words to complete the story.

My baby nephew loves to play with things from the kitchen. He likes the noise they make. When his mother gives him a metal pan or an old tea _____, he squeals with delight. He'll bang on the metal with his _____ or with a wooden spoon. You should hear the clatter he makes!

After a while, he will stop and look around to see if we're enjoying his music. Just when you think he'll _____ down and be quiet, he starts banging again.

His mother laughs at him. She doesn't seem to mind the noise. She says he'll probably be a drummer in a band some day.

Words with *-tle*

beetle	tattle	title	battle
gentle	kettle	settle	rattle

A. Write the correct spelling word beside each clue.

_____ **1.** a metal container for boiling liquids

_____ **2.** to come to rest

_____ **3.** the name of a book or movie

_____ **4.** a toy that makes a noise when it is shaken; or to make short, sharp sounds

_____ **5.** to tell on someone, or to chatter

_____ **6.** an insect

_____ **7.** kind

_____ **8.** fight

B. Write a paragraph using two of the spelling words.

_____

_____

_____

_____

_____

_____

_____

_____

_____

Name_____

LESSON 24   Words with *-tle*

| beetle | tattle | title | battle |
| gentle | kettle | settle | rattle |

A. Write the correct spelling word beside its synonym.

1. fight _____   2. gossip _____

3. name _____   4. mild _____

5. bug _____   6. clatter _____

7. pan _____   8. rest _____

B. Below are pairs of guide words. Write the spelling word that would come between each pair in the dictionary.

_____ 1. head—lame   _____ 2. family—home

_____ 3. team—tone   _____ 4. tall—tavern

_____ 5. bank—bawl

C. Fill in the boxes with the right words.

1. 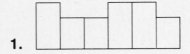   2. 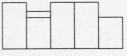   3.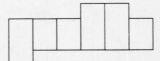

D. Write the spelling words that rhyme with "cattle."

_____   _____   _____

E. Write a spelling word under each picture.

1. _____   2. _____

96

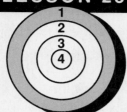

Words with *-kle*

ankle	fickle	buckle	crinkle
tackle	pickle	chuckle	tickle

A. Fill in each blank with a spelling word.

1. A cucumber can be made into a _____.

2. The _____ on my belt is made of brass.

3. I fell on the ice and broke my _____.

4. We're not allowed to play _____ football.

5. Before I finished the joke, I began to _____.

6. A _____ is a kind of wrinkle.

7. People who change their minds often are called _____.

8. We like to _____ our baby sister.

B. Circle the word that is the same as the top one.

ankle	pickle	buckle	crinkle	chuckle	tackle
amkle	pickel	buckle	crinkel	chuckel	tackle
ankel	piekle	buckel	crinkle	ckuckle	tockle
ankle	picklc	bucklc	crirkle	chuckle	tackel
anklc	pickle	buukle	crenkle	chucklc	tackla

C. Fill in the boxes with the right words.

1.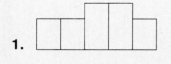

2.

3.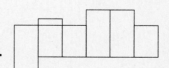

4.

5.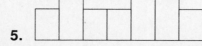

LESSON 25   # Words with *-kle*

ankle	fickle	buckle	crinkle
tackle	pickle	chuckle	tickle

A. Divide each spelling word into syllables on the lines below.

1. ankle _____ _____   2. buckle _____ _____

3. fickle _____ _____   4. pickle _____ _____

5. tackle _____ _____   6. tickle _____ _____

7. chuckle _____ _____   8. crinkle _____ _____

B. Put an *X* on the word that is <u>not</u> the same.

1. ankle	ankle	ankle	ankel	ankle
2. crinkle	cninkle	crinkle	crinkle	crinkle
3. buckle	buckle	buckle	buckle	buckel
4. tackle	tackle	takele	tackle	tackle
5. tickle	tickel	tickle	tickle	tickle

C. Write each word three times.

fickle _____ _____ _____

chuckle _____ _____ _____

pickle _____ _____ _____

ankle _____ _____ _____

tickle _____ _____ _____

D. Write three spelling words that rhyme with each other.

_____   _____   _____

LESSON 25   Words with -kle

ankle	fickle	buckle	crinkle
tackle	pickle	chuckle	tickle

A. Write the correct spelling word beside each clue.

_____ 1. laugh to oneself

_____ 2. the joint that connects the foot and the leg

_____ 3. equipment used for fishing, or to seize or stop

_____ 4. to preserve in a spicy liquid, or a bad situation

_____ 5. likely to change without reason

_____ 6. wrinkle

_____ 7. a fastening, or to bend or crumple

B. Use each spelling word in a sentence.

pickle   _____

tackle   _____

ankle   _____

chuckle   _____

fickle   _____

crinkle   _____

C. Write a spelling word under each picture.

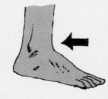      

1. _____   2. _____   3. _____

Name _____

LESSON 25

Words with -kle

ankle	fickle	buckle	crinkle
tackle	pickle	chuckle	tickle

A. Complete these exercises.

1. Write the spelling word that begins with a vowel. _____

2. Which vowel is not in the spelling words? _____

B. One word is wrong in each sentence. Circle the wrong word. Then fill in the blank with a spelling word that makes sense.

1. The runner tripped and broke his tiger.   _____

2. My belt corn is made of silver.   _____

3. Would you like a baseball on your hamburger?   _____

4. We got a cloud out of her joke.   _____

5. The football player made a great eyebrow.   _____

6. If you butter my brother, he'll squeal.   _____

C. Use spelling words to complete the story.

I tried out for the football team today. In one part of the tryout, I was

supposed to _____ the quarterback as he ran toward me. The

quarterback was twice my size.

I was just about to catch him, when I slipped on the grass and fell.

I reached out and grabbed the quarterback's _____. He fell beside

me. "You won't catch me again," he said with a _____. But I did.

I think we'll both make the team.

Words with -ble

thimble	fable	able	mumble
marble	stable	humble	fumble

A. Fill in each blank with a spelling word.

1. The football player may _____ the ball.

2. Put the horse in the _____.

3. I put a _____ on my finger when I sew.

4. "The Fox and the Grapes" is a _____.

5. Will you be _____ to come to my party?

6. I can't understand people when they _____.

7. The building is made of _____.

8. Abe Lincoln lived in a small, _____ log cabin.

B. Circle the word that is the same as the top one.

fable	marble	able	humble	stable	fumble
fabel	manble	abel	hunble	stable	famble
feble	mardle	able	humbel	stabel	fnmble
fable	marbel	adle	humble	stalbe	fumble
falbe	marble	adel	hnmble	stobel	fumbel

C. Write three spelling words with the long *a* sound that rhyme with each other.

_____   _____   _____

D. Below is a pair of guide words. Write the spelling word that would come between the pair in the dictionary.

_____   abide—ankle

Name _____

Words with -ble

thimble	fable	able	mumble
marble	stable	humble	fumble

A. Write the spelling words in alphabetical order.

1. _____ 2. _____ 3. _____ 4. _____

5. _____ 6. _____ 7. _____ 8. _____

B. Use spelling words to complete the story.

After a long ride, my horse and I like to slow down and walk back to the

_____. Yesterday, as we were heading across a field, my horse

stopped, cleared his throat, and said, "I'm awfully thirsty. Could we stop for

a drink of water?"

I couldn't believe my ears! "How long have you been _____ to

talk?" I asked him.

He coughed and sputtered. Then he began to _____. "Please

excuse me," he said, "I haven't talked in so long, I'm a little out of practice.

But I've known how to talk for years."

"For years?" I asked him. "Then why didn't you talk before now?"

"Well," he said, "I was never this thirsty before."

C. Find the missing letters. Then write the word.

1. s ___ ___ ___ ___ ___   _____

2. f ___ ___ ___ ___   _____

3. ___ b ___ ___   _____

LESSON 26   Words with *-ble*

thimble	fable	able	mumble
marble	stable	humble	fumble

A. Divide each spelling word into syllables on the lines below.

1. thimble _____ _____   2. marble _____ _____

3. fable _____ _____   4. stable _____ _____

5. able _____ _____   6. humble _____ _____

7. mumble _____ _____   8. fumble _____ _____

B. Write the correct spelling word beside each clue.

_____ 1. to be clumsy, or to feel about for something with the hands

_____ 2. steady, or a place where horses and cattle are kept

_____ 3. to speak in a low and unclear way

_____ 4. simple, or modest

_____ 5. a smooth, hard stone

_____ 6. a fairy tail, or a story that teaches a lesson

C. Write the correct spelling word beside its synonym.

1. myth _____   2. capable _____

3. drop _____   4. barn _____

5. modest _____   6. mutter _____

D. Write the spelling words that begin with two consonants.

_____ _____

Words with -ble

thimble	fable	able	mumble
marble	stable	humble	fumble

A. Complete these exercises.

1. Circle the vowels that are in the spelling words.

    a   e   i   o   u

2. Which spelling word is the longest? _____

3. In which spelling words can the letters *a, b, l,* and *e* be found?

    _____   _____

    _____   _____

4. Which spelling word contains two *m*'s?

    _____

5. Which spelling words don't rhyme with other spelling words?

    _____   _____

B. Write a paragraph using two of the spelling words.

_____

_____

_____

_____

_____

_____

_____

_____

LESSON 27   Words with *-gle*

single	bugle	gargle	juggle
struggle	jingle	giggle	jungle

A. Fill in each blank with a spelling word.

1. When she heard the joke, she began to _____.

2. Each morning the soldiers awaken to a _____.

3. We had to _____ to keep the canoe afloat.

4. My sister and I have _____ beds.

5. You should _____ to make your sore throat feel better.

6. I heard the bells _____.

7. The clown can _____ six oranges at once.

8. In Asia, tigers live in the _____.

B. Write the spelling words in alphabetical order.

1. _____ 2. _____ 3. _____ 4. _____

5. _____ 6. _____ 7. _____ 8. _____

C. Fill in the boxes with the right words.

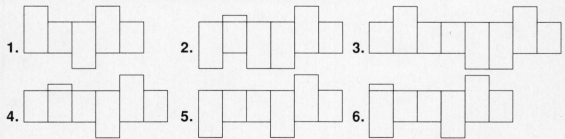

1.   2.   3.

4.   5.   6.

D. Write the correct spelling word beside its synonym.

1. laugh _____   2. horn _____

3. one _____   4. fight _____

Name _____

Words with *-gle*

single	bugle	gargle	juggle
struggle	jingle	giggle	jungle

A. Put an *X* on the word that is <u>not</u> the same.

1. single	single	single	single	singel
2. bugle	dugle	bugle	bugle	bugle
3. giggle	giggle	giggle	giqqle	giggle
4. gargle	gargle	gurgle	gargle	gargle
5. jungle	junjle	jungle	jungle	jungle

B. Divide each spelling word into syllables on the lines below.

1. single _____ _____   2. struggle _____ _____

3. bugle _____ _____   4. jingle _____ _____

5. gargle _____ _____   6. giggle _____ _____

7. juggle _____ _____   8. jungle _____ _____

C. Write a spelling word under each picture.

1. _____   2. _____   3. _____

D. Write two spelling words that contain *in*.

_____   _____

Words with -gle

single	bugle	gargle	juggle
struggle	jingle	giggle	jungle

A. Write the correct spelling word beside each clue.

_____ **1.** the sound of a bell

_____ **2.** a musical instrument like a small trumpet

_____ **3.** to laugh in a silly way

_____ **4.** to rinse the throat with a liquid kept in motion by the breath

_____ **5.** only one, or not married

_____ **6.** to make a great effort, or fighting

_____ **7.** to keep balls in the air by tossing and catching them quickly

_____ **8.** wild land overgrown with bushes and trees

B. Use each spelling word in a sentence.

struggle _____

gargle _____

single _____

juggle _____

bugle _____

jingle _____

jungle _____

giggle _____

Name _____

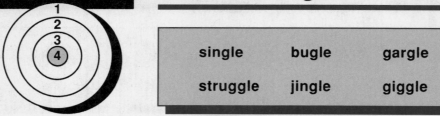

LESSON 27

Words with *-gle*

single	bugle	gargle	juggle
struggle	jingle	giggle	jungle

A. Below are pairs of guide words. Write the spelling word that would come between each pair in the dictionary.

_____ **1.** gather—gurgle

_____ **2.** sandy—song

_____ **3.** juggling—Jupiter

_____ **4.** brain—butter

B. Write each word three times.

juggle _____ _____ _____

giggle _____ _____ _____

struggle _____ _____ _____

single _____ _____ _____

gargle _____ _____ _____

bugle _____ _____ _____

jingle _____ _____ _____

jungle _____ _____ _____

C. Use spelling words to complete the story.

Each fall our town has a big parade. We start making the floats in the

summer. But it's still a _____ to have them ready on time.

The best float this year has over twenty cardboard trees. There are

monkeys and rubber snakes hanging from the trees. It looks like a scene

from the _____.

108

LESSON 28

Words with *-le*

rifle	nozzle	waffle	vehicle
drizzle	example	sample	bicycle

A. Fill in each blank with a spelling word.

1. Let's do an _____ from the homework together.

2. Here is a _____ of the cloth I picked.

3. A jeep is a kind of _____.

4. A _____ has wheels with spokes.

5. I learned how to shoot a _____ at camp.

6. The _____ on my hose is leaking.

7. The rainstorm began as a _____.

8. Do you like your _____ with butter and syrup?

B. Find the missing letters. Then write the word.

1. e x __ __ __ __ __   _____

2. __ __ __ f __ __   _____

3. __ r __ __ __ __ __   _____

4. __ __ f __ __   _____

5. __ __ h __ c __ __   _____

C. Write the spelling words in alphabetical order.

1. _____   2. _____   3. _____

4. _____   5. _____   6. _____

7. _____   8. _____

Name _____

Words with -le

rifle	nozzle	waffle	vehicle
drizzle	example	sample	bicycle

A. **Divide each spelling word into syllables on the lines below.**

1. rifle _____ _____

2. drizzle _____ _____

3. nozzle _____ _____

4. example _____ _____ _____

5. waffle _____ _____

6. sample _____ _____

7. vehicle _____ _____ _____

8. bicycle _____ _____ _____

B. **Complete these exercises with spelling words.**

1. The first four letters of this word mean "test." _____

2. This is usually eaten for breakfast. _____

3. The first two letters of this word spell "no." _____

4. This word has five consonants. _____

C. **Use spelling words to complete the story.**

Last week my brother and I made breakfast for our mother.

Early one morning, I rode my _____ to the store to buy the

food we needed. I got a carton of milk, a dozen eggs, and some

_____ mix. The box had a free _____ of syrup attached

to it.

As I was riding home from the store, it began to _____. Soon it

was raining hard. By the time I got home, the waffle mix was soaked. So

we made scrambled eggs instead of waffles. They turned out great. Our

mother thanked us for making her day special.

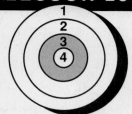

LESSON 28

Words with *-le*

rifle	nozzle	waffle	vehicle
drizzle	example	sample	bicycle

A. Circle the word that is the same as the top one.

rifle	drizzle	sample	waffle	vehicle	bicycle
rifel	drizzel	sample	waffel	venicle	bycicle
rifle	drizle	simple	wafle	vericle	bicycle
rilfe	dnizle	sampel	walffe	vahicle	bilcycle
nifle	drizzle	sanple	waffle	vehicle	bicicle

B. Use spelling words to complete the puzzle.

Across

4. light rain

6. A car is a kind of ___.

7. a sample or model

Down

1. It sprays water.

2. a vehicle with two wheels

3. a kind of breakfast food

5. a type of gun

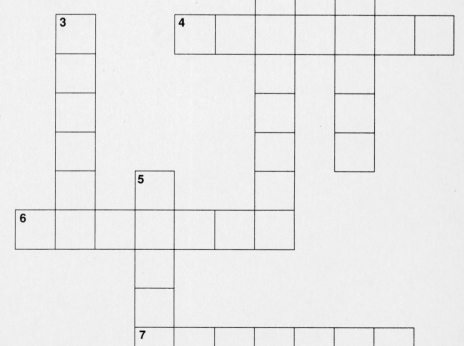

Name _____

111

LESSON 28   Words with -le

rifle	nozzle	waffle	vehicle
drizzle	example	sample	bicycle

A. Write a spelling word under each picture.

   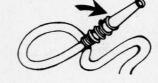   

1. _____   2. _____   3. _____

B. Write the correct spelling word beside each clue.

_____ 1. very light rain, like mist

_____ 2. a kind of spout on the end of a hose

_____ 3. a metal frame with two wheels, handles for steering, and a seat for the rider

_____ 4. a gun with a long barrel

_____ 5. an airplane, truck, car, or any other means of carrying people or goods

C. Write a paragraph using two of the spelling words.

_____

_____

_____

_____

_____

_____

_____

_____

112

Homonyms

scene	weak	steel	beat
seen	week	steal	beet

A. Fill in each blank with a spelling word.

1. There are seven days in a _____.

2. The root of a _____ is cooked and eaten.

3. I painted a beach _____.

4. He's feeling _____ from not eating breakfast.

5. The frame of the building is made of _____.

6. Did the burglar _____ any silver?

7. Their team _____ ours in the game last night.

8. Have you ever _____ snow?

B. Write the spelling words that rhyme with the words below.

1. seat   feet   _____

2. green   bean   _____

3. meal   feel   _____

4. leak   peek   _____

C. Find the missing letters. Then write the word.

1. ___ c ___ ___ ___   _____

2. ___ ___ e t   _____

3. ___ ___ a t   _____

4. ___ ___ a k   _____

Homonyms

scene	weak	steel	beat
seen	week	steal	beet

A. Write the correct spelling word beside each clue.

_____ 1. a view or picture, or show of strong emotion in front of others

_____ 2. to take something that does not belong to one

_____ 3. a form of "to see"

_____ 4. a strong, hard metal made from iron mixed with carbon

_____ 5. lacking strength or health

_____ 6. to strike or whip again and again, or a unit of time in music

_____ 7. the seven days from Sunday to Saturday

_____ 8. a red root eaten as a vegetable

B. Use each spelling word in a sentence.

scene _____

weak _____

steal _____

beat _____

seen _____

steel _____

week _____

beet _____

Homonyms

scene	weak	steel	beat
seen	week	steal	beet

A. Write the spelling words in alphabetical order.

1. _____ 2. _____ 3. _____ 4. _____

5. _____ 6. _____ 7. _____ 8. _____

B. Write the correct spelling word beside its synonym.

1. whip _____ 2. rob _____

3. setting _____ 4. feeble _____

C. Put an *X* on the word that is <u>not</u> the same.

1. weak	weak	weak	weck	weak
2. steal	steal	steal	steal	stael
3. seen	sein	seen	seen	seen
4. beat	beat	beet	beat	beat
5. scene	scene	scene	sceen	scene
6. week	week	week	weik	week
7. steel	steil	steel	steel	steel
8. beet	beet	beet	beet	deet

D. Complete these exercises with spelling words.

1. Which word has a silent *c*? _____

2. Which words do not have two *e*'s?

_____ _____ _____

Name _____

Homonyms

scene	weak	steel	beat
seen	week	steal	beet

A. Use spelling words to complete the story.

Last _____ on my favorite TV show, there was a _____

that took place in a bank. A robber walks into the bank. He hands the teller

a note that says, "Give me all your money."

The teller has _____ the robber before. He's one of her

neighbors. She pushes an alarm by her foot that brings the police to the

bank. They arrest the robber. The teller wonders why her neighbor would try

to _____ money from the bank.

B. Below are pairs of guide words. Write the spelling word that would come between each pair in the dictionary.

_____ 1. stare—steam

_____ 2. sail—seat

_____ 3. weed—weird

_____ 4. bear—beaver

_____ 5. see—sent

C. Circle the word that is the same as the top one.

scene	weak	steel	beat	steal	seen
sceen	week	steel	beet	steel	sene
scene	waek	steal	beat	stael	sceen
secne	weke	stele	baet	steal	seer
scenc	weak	stecl	bete	steol	seen

Words with *-ey*

monkey	journey	turkey	hockey
pulley	valley	chimney	jersey

A. Fill in each blank with a spelling word.

1. We drove down into the _____.

2. I saw smoke rising from the house's _____.

3. Have you seen ice _____ being played?

4. We often eat _____ on Thanksgiving.

5. That _____ loves to eat bananas.

6. The flag is raised by the use of a _____.

7. Our _____ was by bus.

8. The football player has a new yellow _____.

B. Divide each spelling word into syllables on the lines below.

1. monkey _____ _____   2. journey _____ _____

3. turkey _____ _____   4. hockey _____ _____

5. pulley _____ _____   6. valley _____ _____

7. chimney _____ _____   8. jersey _____ _____

C. Write a spelling word under each picture.

1. _____   2. _____   3. _____

Name _____

LESSON 30

Words with -ey

monkey	journey	turkey	hockey
pulley	valley	chimney	jersey

A. Circle the word that is the same as the top one.

chimney	jersey	monkey	valley	hockey	journey
ckimney	jensey	mnokey	valely	hochey	journey
chimmey	jersey	monkee	valley	hokey	jounrey
chinmey	gersey	monkey	vattey	hackey	juonrey
chimney	jirsey	monhey	vallay	kockey	jounney
chimley	gernsey	morkey	valliey	hockey	jurney

B. Use spelling words to complete the story.

Once upon a time, a _____ ran away from the zoo. He was tired

of living in a small space. And he was tired of so many visitors. He wanted

to be free.

For days he wandered around. His _____ took him a long way

from the zoo. He began to feel tired and hungry. Soon he saw a large

house standing alone in a _____. Smoke was coming from its

brick _____.

He knocked on the door. A woman opened it. She was surprised to see

a monkey. "I'm very hungry," said the monkey.

The woman was even more surprised to hear the monkey talk. She

shared her family's _____ dinner with the monkey. When the family

invited the monkey to stay with them, he said yes. He had a long and happy

life with the family.

Words with -ey

monkey	journey	turkey	hockey
pulley	valley	chimney	jersey

A. Write the correct spelling word beside each clue.

_____ 1. low land between two mountains

_____ 2. a large bird commonly raised for food

_____ 3. a small mammal

_____ 4. a wheel turned by a rope used to lift heavy objects

_____ 5. a trip

_____ 6. the part of a building that smoke escapes from

_____ 7. soft, knitted cloth; or a garment for the upper body

_____ 8. a game played on ice or on a field

B. Write a paragraph using two of the spelling words.

_____

_____

_____

_____

_____

_____

_____

C. Write the correct spelling word beside its synonym.

1. shirt _____   2. smokestack _____

3. ape _____   4. trip _____

Name _____

LESSON 30

Words with *-ey*

monkey	journey	turkey	hockey
pulley	valley	chimney	jersey

A. **Find the missing letters. Then write the word.**

1. __ o u __ __ __ __   _____

2. __ a l __ __ __   _____

3. t __ r __ __ __   _____

4. j __ __ __ __ __   _____

B. **Complete these exercises.**

1. Which spelling words contain the word "key"?

_____   _____   _____

2. Circle the vowels that are in the spelling words.

a   e   i   o   u

3. Which spelling word would you find first in the dictionary?

_____

4. Which spelling word is also a country?

_____

C. **Fill in the boxes with the right words.**

1. 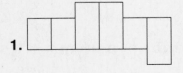   2.    3.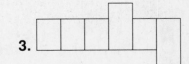

4.    5.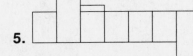

120

My Word List

Words I Can Spell

Put a ✓ in the box beside each word you spell correctly on your weekly test.

1

- ☐ around
- ☐ agree
- ☐ alone
- ☐ avoid
- ☐ above
- ☐ afraid
- ☐ awake
- ☐ amaze

2

- ☐ rocket
- ☐ ticket
- ☐ jacket
- ☐ market
- ☐ pocket
- ☐ racket
- ☐ socket
- ☐ closet

3

- ☐ brother
- ☐ other
- ☐ mother
- ☐ another
- ☐ father
- ☐ bother
- ☐ farther
- ☐ either

4

- ☐ do
- ☐ dew
- ☐ knight
- ☐ night
- ☐ sight
- ☐ site
- ☐ wade
- ☐ weighed

5

- ☐ coming
- ☐ having
- ☐ using
- ☐ loving
- ☐ living
- ☐ hoping
- ☐ biting
- ☐ making

Words To Review

If you miss a word on your test, write it here. Practice it until you can spell it correctly. Then check the box beside the word.

_____

_____

_____

_____

_____

_____

_____

_____

_____

_____

_____

_____

_____

_____

_____

_____

_____

_____

_____

_____

Name _____

My Word List

Words I Can Spell

Put a ✓ in the box beside each word you spell correctly on your weekly test.

6

☐ dropping   ☐ hopping
☐ shipping   ☐ stripping
☐ pinning   ☐ canning
☐ humming   ☐ stopping

7

☐ wiper   ☐ voter
☐ diner   ☐ skater
☐ shaver   ☐ glider
☐ giver   ☐ ruler

8

☐ mail   ☐ wrap
☐ male   ☐ rap
☐ whole   ☐ buy
☐ hole   ☐ by

9

☐ zipper   ☐ clipper
☐ slipper   ☐ chopper
☐ dropper   ☐ jogger
☐ winner   ☐ shopper

10

☐ scraped   ☐ chased
☐ timed   ☐ filed
☐ hiked   ☐ closed
☐ used   ☐ moved

Words To Review

If you miss a word on your test, write it here. Practice it until you can spell it correctly. Then check the box beside the word.

_____

_____

_____

_____

_____

_____

_____

_____

_____

_____

_____

_____

_____

_____

_____

_____

_____

My Word List

Words I Can Spell

Put a ✓ in the box beside each word you spell correctly on your weekly test.

11

☐ ripped   ☐ stepped
☐ hopped   ☐ dropped
☐ shipped   ☐ scrubbed
☐ canned   ☐ slammed

12

☐ wear   ☐ which
☐ where   ☐ witch
☐ weather   ☐ heard
☐ whether   ☐ herd

13

☐ phrase   ☐ photo
☐ telephone   ☐ alphabet
☐ geography   ☐ elephant
☐ sphere   ☐ nephew

14

☐ smaller   ☐ thicker
☐ fresher   ☐ stronger
☐ smarter   ☐ cheaper
☐ quicker   ☐ older

15

☐ softest   ☐ quickest
☐ warmest   ☐ sharpest
☐ cleanest   ☐ brightest
☐ neatest   ☐ poorest

Words To Review

If you miss a word on your test, write it here. Practice it until you can spell it correctly. Then check the box beside the word.

_____
_____
_____
_____
_____
_____
_____
_____
_____
_____
_____
_____
_____
_____
_____
_____
_____

Name _____

My Word List

Words I Can Spell

Put a ✓ in the box beside each word you spell correctly on your weekly test.

16

☐ clever   ☐ silver
☐ whisper   ☐ corner
☐ chapter   ☐ wander
☐ cover   ☐ enter

17

☐ pour   ☐ deer
☐ pore   ☐ dear
☐ won   ☐ meat
☐ one   ☐ meet

18

☐ rescue   ☐ argue
☐ avenue   ☐ continue
☐ statue   ☐ glue
☐ true   ☐ clue

19

☐ trial   ☐ dial
☐ normal   ☐ pedal
☐ metal   ☐ formal
☐ personal   ☐ editorial

20

☐ cruel   ☐ fuel
☐ jewel   ☐ bushel
☐ towel   ☐ barrel
☐ duel   ☐ vowel

Words To Review

If you miss a word on your test, write it here. Practice it until you can spell it correctly. Then check the box beside the word.

_____

_____

_____

_____

_____

_____

_____

_____

_____

_____

_____

_____

_____

_____

My Word List

Words I Can Spell

Put a ✓ in the box beside each word you spell correctly on your weekly test.

21

☐ staple   ☐ purple
☐ apple   ☐ steeple
☐ maple   ☐ simple
☐ people   ☐ cable

22

☐ cradle   ☐ poodle
☐ needle   ☐ riddle
☐ middle   ☐ handle
☐ peddle   ☐ saddle

23

☐ pain   ☐ led
☐ pane   ☐ lead
☐ wood   ☐ break
☐ would   ☐ brake

24

☐ beetle   ☐ title
☐ gentle   ☐ settle
☐ tattle   ☐ battle
☐ kettle   ☐ rattle

25

☐ ankle   ☐ buckle
☐ tackle   ☐ chuckle
☐ fickle   ☐ crinkle
☐ pickle   ☐ tickle

Words To Review

If you miss a word on your test, write it here. Practice it until you can spell it correctly. Then check the box beside the word.

_____

_____

_____

_____

_____

_____

_____

_____

_____

_____

_____

_____

_____

_____

_____

_____

_____

© 1991 Steck-Vaughn Company. Target 1020

Name _____

My Word List

Words I Can Spell

Put a ✓ in the box beside each word you spell correctly on your weekly test.

26

☐ thimble	☐ able
☐ marble	☐ humble
☐ fable	☐ mumble
☐ stable	☐ fumble

27

☐ single	☐ gargle
☐ struggle	☐ giggle
☐ bugle	☐ juggle
☐ jingle	☐ jungle

28

☐ rifle	☐ waffle
☐ drizzle	☐ sample
☐ nozzle	☐ vehicle
☐ example	☐ bicycle

29

☐ scene	☐ steel
☐ seen	☐ steal
☐ weak	☐ beat
☐ week	☐ beet

30

☐ monkey	☐ turkey
☐ pulley	☐ chimney
☐ journey	☐ hockey
☐ valley	☐ jersey

Words To Review

If you miss a word on your test, write it here. Practice it until you can spell it correctly. Then check the box beside the word.

_____

_____

_____

_____

_____

_____

_____

_____

_____

_____

_____

_____

_____

_____

_____